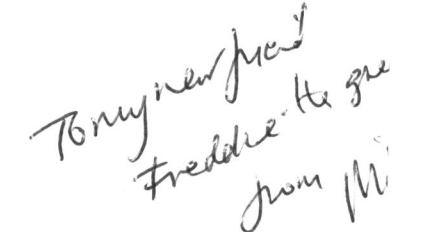

Don't Upset Renee

The discovery of emotional oppression

Michael Sylvester
with David Knight

Copyright © 2010 Michael Sylvester

Reprinted December 2013
Reprinted February 2015
Reprinted March 2016

Michael Sylvester is hereby identified as author of this work in accordance with Section 77 of the Copyright, Designs and Patent Act 1988.

Apart from any fair dealing for the purposes of research or private study, or criticism or review, as permitted under the Copyright, Designs and Patents Act 1988, this publication may only be reproduced, stored or transmitted, in any form or by any means, with the prior permission in writing of the publishers, or in the case of reprographic reproduction in accordance with the terms of licences issued by the Copyright Licensing Agency. Enquiries concerning reproduction outside those terms should be sent to the publishers.

Matador
9 Priory Business Park
Wistow Road
Kibworth
Leicester LE8 0RX, UK
Tel: 01162792299
Email: books@troubador.co.uk
Web: www.troubador.co.uk/matador

ISBN 978-184876-407-1

A Cataloguing-in-Publication (CIP) catalogue record for this book is available from the British Library.

Cover illustration by Alex Bennett, Design Jungle, Leicester

Typeset in 11pt Book Antiqua by Troubador Publishing Ltd, Leicester, UK

Matador is an imprint of Troubador Publishing Ltd

Acknowledgements

To Anne

Who can find a good woman?
She is precious beyond all things
Her husband's heart trusts her completely
She is his best reward
Proverbs 31 v10-11

David Knight

Thank you David for your tenacious questioning, focus and time. You have been able to translate the orator's story into a book of learning for others.

Michael Sylvester is 69 years old and lives with his wife Anne in Nottinghamshire. He started his own business as a chartered marketer, sales trainer and mentor in 1986. Mike has worked in government, corporate business and the not-for-profit sectors helping people to develop business skills.

Having left school with no qualifications, Mike was awarded a Fellowship in 2006 by the Chartered Institute of Marketing for his contribution to the subject since 1982.

Mike's hobbies and interests include physical exercise, cooking and gardening. When time allows, he can be found on the River Trent, relaxing on his boat named 'Motivator'.

David Knight is a former newspaper editor and television publicity officer who set up his own writing and design company, Writers Editorial Services, in 1990. He is also a part-time lecturer in journalism.

Contents

- vii   Prologue: Horses for courses
- 1   Could have tried harder
- 5   Renee Petite
- 9   Don't upset Renee
- 15   School caps, rubbed collars and unfastened blouses
- 21   Packhoss
- 29   Bully for Michael
- 37   Life of a salesman
- 43   Letdown
- 47   The odd number
- 53   The curse of 'getting there'
- 61   The divine leap
- 67   Emotional oppression and unconditional approval
- 73   From the Bottom up
- 79   Bullying – the last stand
- 85   The butcher and the butcher's boy
- 93   Goodnight Irene
- 101   Going around in circles

PROLOGUE

Horses for courses

There's an old English proverb: 'You can lead a horse to water, but you can't make it drink'. Supported by the experiences I am going to share with you in this book, I hope you will gain a new insight from this saying. I hope you will see from some of the work I have developed as a salesman, manager, trainer and mentor that the key point is not necessarily trying to make the horse drink. I have found (and it's the focus of my current projects), that the purpose of the task is to make it feel thirsty.

I feel I have endured and overcome many emotions and challenges, which it has taken me years to understand. It's as if I have lived my life against a constant conflicting backdrop – of one voice saying 'you can't, you're not allowed', and of another countering 'I bloody can, I'll find a way'. It sounds like a running battle. I would describe it more as an ever–present disturbance. I know that I am by no means alone in feeling this.

I've managed the effects of it to some degree by spiritual beliefs and physical disciplines. At one time, I got a lot of out of my system by running. It's noticeable that, for the most part, I have concentrated on individual sport – on my own, facing the struggle, only joining others every now and then to form a team. When I considered myself no longer able to continue regular running, I took on gym work. Here again, I face my challenges on my own, but I also draw upon the camaraderie of other people from different environments striving to reach their own personal goals.

Professionally speaking, the major years of my personal insight emerged after I had taken the decision to become self–

employed, to follow what I wanted to do, what I thought I was good at, instead of what conditioning taught me I should do, or had to do, or what others thought it would be best for me to do.

In my early self–employed years, the residential management training programmes that I used to help organise and run laid down a framework for my learning.

The momentum, or rhythm, of the course went like this. . .

On the first day of the three–day residential programme, we would introduce attendees to the concept of the course, and how it would embrace their workplace roles. We also worked on creating an atmosphere under which the attendees could share and understand each other's views. Quite often, people came with competitive views on a subject. Sales management was always complicated to get under way because people had marked views based on their experiences and interpretations.

Egos also intruded – 'I'm the salesman, now I'm the manager, now I'm better than everyone else' – and that always took a lot of time to sort out. Without encouragement to overcome differences of opinion, or of cultures, it would not be possible for us to set the evening exercise for the first day. As well as setting the exercise, we would encourage them to eat together and have a few drinks.

On the second day, the group would begin to gel and to enjoy each other's company. They would give me a demonstration on their findings from the previous evening's study and we would then 'wash that up' with a discussion. Then we would broaden out the subject we were studying, whether it be sales management or marketing. We would explore certain areas chosen by the group, moving into describing situations instead of it being about explanation all the time. We would finish with another exercise, making it as light–hearted as possible.

The third day would start with the 'wash up' from that exercise.

And I would go on to challenge the delegates – in a non-hostile way – to get out the door and get back to work and try out what they had learned, to discover what happens.

We usually found that the attendees couldn't wait to get back the next day and put in place an appraisal plan, or interview someone, or go out and see a customer, or rewrite their marketing spiel... the list was endless.

We had made them thirsty.

Why am I explaining this? I'm following the same pattern with my contents of this book. You will see that I go into 'this is what happened to me' and, once I have described it, review and discuss what it has meant to me.

Have you got anything like this you know? Does your family have a similar situation? I'm not saying my reactions and insights are correct or universal, I'm not saying the problems we face are scientific. This is not a self-help book. I'm just saying 'look at this, look at what happened to me' and most people I talk to about my story say 'you know that's really interesting', 'that's happened to me'.

I don't want people to say 'tell me what I can do'. I am simply saying 'here's something you can think about'. Go and play with it and see if there's anything in it.

If you don't, it may become a case of 'could have tried harder'...

Here's to you, as good as you are
And to me, as bad as I am
But as good as you are,
and as bad as I am,
I'm as good as you are. . .
(as bad as I am)

Les Sylvester 1907-2000

CHAPTER ONE

Could have tried harder

Rise or fall. Hit the heights, or plumb the depths. There's only one way up and one way down, I was led to believe, when it comes to 'being successful' in life.

It conjures up a picture of the fairground attraction 'trial of strength'. In front of you, a fixed upright scale identifying all the different levels of achievement. At the base, a platform or disc – the target area for your hammer blow. Your success will be measured by how hard you manage to strike the base, and trigger the reaction of the target object up towards the pinnacle of a bell.

Imagine you're being watched. If the bell sounds, you receive acclaim and admiration. You have the abilities you should have. If the target object falls short, you receive sighs, or perhaps muffled amusement, or even open derision from those around you.

The only thing you can do to sound the bell and gain acceptance – despite your weight, your height, your strength, your intuition – is to hammer away at the target area harder and harder and harder still.

'Could have tried harder'. That's what they always said about me in reports at the end of school terms.

I received a private education, the best my dad could afford at mother's insistence. Yet when I left, I had no qualifications or knowledge of how to question or listen. I had no ability to read and I could not speak another language. I could not even interpret body language. I had no understanding of the opposite sex. I could not cope with challenge or conflict. I had never visited another country and I had no racial or cultural awareness.

All that school had effectively equipped me with was the knowledge that I was English – the best country in the world, the leader of the empire – and that I was ready for the outside world because I was a representative of a privileged educational background.

In this great nation, with its vertical thinking and view of success, my school uniform gave the impression I was at the top.

Deep down, I knew I was actually at the bottom. These were the only clothes I had. It would take me more than 20 years to realise that hammering away at a single target area harder and harder – an area defined by someone else – could only ever lead to frustration and narrow achievement in life.

'Could have tried harder'. Not the most harmful phrase, you might think. Indeed, there is a saying: 'Sticks and stones may break my bones, but words will never hurt me'. What I have come to learn, though, is that an everyday phrase can hurt you. Depending on how and when it's said, it can have a lifetime's consequences.

It needn't be 'could have tried harder'. It could be any one of hundreds of so–called 'throwaway' remarks – 'who do you think you are', 'get a grip of yourself', 'you don't realise how lucky you are', 'pull yourself together', 'you don't know the meaning of stressed/tired/depressed', 'it never did me any harm'.

In my case, it was 'could have tried harder'. And as I have travelled the country in my role as a business mentor, I have been amazed at the number of times this particular phrase has reared up in conversation with others.

The English language is a complex construct. If we bothered to consult a dictionary or a grammar book, we would realise we're not often saying literally what we think we are saying. Nevertheless, consciously or subconsciously, we choose and use particular words to convey feeling and effect.

There was a popular song in the Noughties called 'Shoulda Woulda Coulda'. It made me wonder how, if the alternatives in this title were applied, it would affect the phrase that has haunted me.

It's hard to imagine being told we 'would have' tried harder, because it doesn't make immediate sense. The phrase seems incomplete. It requires a disclaimer: 'You would have tried harder if. . .' And that 'if' carries an implication that it might have required some input on behalf of the person making the observation. Perhaps it's not said because they may be reluctant to bring themselves into the equation.

Imagine if the message had been we 'should have' tried harder. That doesn't sound so bad. It carries the implication that we made the effort but it might have been misplaced. It feels as though the commentator is speaking from a position of shared concern: it sounds advisory, and leaves open the possibility of another chance. It leaves you with more of an impression that the person making the comment is not completely against you.

But we were told we 'could have' tried harder. It carries the cold implication that we didn't bother to make any effort: we wilfully chose to go against our talent and potential. It's subjective, judgmental and dismissive. And, for some reason, like mud that's been thrown, it seems to stick. It spreads as a slur on our general attitude instead of just being a comment about a particular instance.

It makes us more of a victim than 'would have' or 'should have'. It is designed to make us feel bad about a situation or, more to the point, ourselves.

'Could have' is a tell–tale sign that someone wants to put us down, put us in 'our place' – somewhere we needn't think we're so special or clever.

So it makes you think, what sort of person wants to make another person feel that bad?

CHAPTER TWO

Renee Petite

Renee Petite was sweet 16 when she first met Les Sylvester at the Clock Tower in Skegness. They were each on holiday at the Lincolnshire seaside resort – Les, six years older, was with his family and Renee was visiting with the Guides.

It was the end of the 1920s. Unemployment was high following the Wall Street crash, but it was also an exciting time with booming housing and leisure industries – particularly at the cinema, where a new era of 'talkies' had begun.

Renee had lost her father, Joe, when she was five. A man of Irish descent, he had been both a soldier and seaman in the First World War and had become a fireman on his return. But it had been none of these hazardous occupations that had claimed his life. Joe fell to the 1919 'flu epidemic which swept Europe and killed millions whose resistance had been fatally weakened by the conflict.

One of Renee's earliest memories is of being lifted onto Joe's knee when she was about two and recoiling at the itchiness of his khaki uniform.

After she lost her father, Renee was sent to the country to be brought up by her Auntie Ethel and Uncle Len – her mother's sister and brother–in–law. Ethel and Len lived in the Nottinghamshire village of Epperstone. Renee remembers it as the best time of her life.

After about two years, another little girl came to live at the house. They played together and made friends. Then Renee was told that her playmate was actually her sister, Marjorie.

Renee and Marjorie's mother, Anne, was known for having a series of relationships. Renee can recall one visit to a Nottingham cinema house when she and Marjorie watched a feature three times in a row because Anne was with the projectionist in the back room.

In her teens, Renee moved back to live with her mother in Nottingham and attended the convent school in Derby Road. Anne had met and settled down with a relatively wealthy man called JW. He came from a farming family in Collingham, near Newark, and owned a small confectionery warehouse in the city.

One day in her new home, Renee opened a cupboard door and discovered a half–eaten wedding cake. It was the first she knew of her mother having become married again.

Shortly afterwards, Renee's mother and JW took in a lodger known as 'Buzzy', who had moved to Nottingham from east London. 'Buzzy' was originally from Russia and had sailed to England with thousands of other refugees at the time of the Russian Revolution.

JW helped 'Buzzy' to find his feet by giving him a job in his confectionery warehouse. 'Buzzy' returned the compliment by taking JW's place in Anne's bed. Suddenly, JW had departed the scene. Anne and 'Buzzy' had taken over his bank accounts, the warehouse and a shop.

The number of shops increased to half a dozen as 'Buzzy' built a tobacco and sweets empire in Nottingham. His influence spread even further afield. He provided all confectionery free of charge to Nottinghamshire Constabulary Christmas ball. He went along to fairs across the country – including Nottingham's famous Goose Fair – to collect money from stallholders. He carried a gun.

Renee accompanied 'Buzzy' when he drove to Coventry on

one of his missions. She was in the car when she heard the crack of gunshots. 'Buzzy' was hit twice. Later, it was explained to Renee that 'Buzzy' had shot himself in an attempt to claim insurance.

After their Skegness Clock Tower encounter, Renee and Les returned to Nottingham and began courting. To protect his new–found and dearly–held relationship, Les was keen not to alienate 'Buzzy' or his family. One of 'Buzzy's' brothers visited the city and Les tried to befriend him. They were walking through Nottingham one day when a policeman approached Les and warned him: 'Have nothing to do with this man. Get away from him. Have nothing to do with him whatsoever'.

Renee worked in one of the sweet shops owned by 'Buzzy' until her late teens before it came to an abrupt halt. She was forced to leave both the job and her home as Anne and 'Buzzy' departed Nottingham and moved to London to develop the confectionery business in league with a number of new acquaintances, reputedly including the Kray twins.

Renee took a job at the Nottingham department store of Griffin & Spalding and, having nowhere else to live, was taken in by Les's sister, Dorothy. Two years before the outbreak of the Second World War, Renee and Les were married. They set up home in Toton, on the outskirts of Nottingham.

The newlyweds were reunited – very briefly – with 'Buzzy' during the war years. Seemingly oblivious to the shortage of petrol, 'Buzzy' took a taxi from London to Toton one day with a complete set of company books in his possession. Upon arrival, Les dug a hole in the field next to his house. 'Buzzy' dropped the paperwork into the hole and set fire to it. 'Buzzy' promptly covered over the hole, got back into the taxi and returned to London.

'Buzzy' sold his business to another East End group and moved with Anne to Southend 'to escape the bombing'.

Anne and 'Buzzy' were to return together to Nottingham some years later. In the meantime, on 6 December 1946, almost ten years after becoming Mrs Sylvester, Renee gave birth to a son, Michael.

CHAPTER THREE

Don't Upset Renee

I've been told that Renee Sylvester was a loving and caring mother and that, when I was very young, she looked after me extraordinarily well. I was cosseted, almost wrapped up in wool.

Yet I have always carried the impression that, in her eyes, I was never any good at anything – that I could do nothing to come up to the standards she imagined for me.

As I've gone through life, I have managed to overcome a sense of inadequacy and an inability to handle my emotions – both of which I link to mother. I have recognised that, in moments of emotional challenge, I just wanted to go away and cry. Then I wanted to be vengeful, to get my own back. This all goes back to mother.

It has made me realise that, no matter how old or experienced we are, the negative culture and thoughts that some parents and guardians plant in our heads when we are children stay forever, eating away at everything positive we want to do. It is so painful in the conditioning of our lives.

When I think of mother's life and experiences, there's a part of me that says she couldn't do anything about what happened to her or how she reacted. But the other part is a concern about how much damage she has done to me in the process.

I said that I'd been told Renee was loving and caring. It was Auntie Gwen, my dad's younger sister, who told me. She also told me that mother and dad loved me. Neither mother nor dad ever told me themselves.

But I loved my dad. He worked as a butcher with the Co-op for 50 years. He was a big favourite with his customers and respected by his fellow workers. He was their union convenor and his loyalty to the union was rewarded with free life membership. Les Sylvester knew his role in life. He was careful with his money, played cricket, football and boxed. He had an enormous and infectious sense of fun and humour.

One of the earliest stories about me is when I was five years old. The school inspector called at our house. Mother had kept me from classes because it was cold. I've presumed this to be the reason for the impression I grew up with that I was delicate, a weakling. This was annually reinforced by the fact I was bedridden every July for two weeks because of asthma – although mother never referred to it as asthma, because she regarded it as a weakness. I was given an extra vest to wear and she would tell people that I had 'a summer cold'. Actually, we have since found out that I was allergic to the mould that formed on crops in the fields outside our home.

Another feeling that's stayed with me since those early years is of a sense of exclusion.

At the age of six, I was sent to stay with my aunt and uncle for three weeks when mother went into hospital. She was seriously ill. After she was allowed out, everyone gathered to welcome her back home. I was sent to play in next door's garden. There was no one else in the street. I can still remember the little yellow and orange Dinky toy I was given to play with. I remember seeing mother getting out of the taxi and my dad and my granddad coming out to hug her. My aunts and uncles were also there and I didn't know what was happening.

Renee had been pregnant again. But she had lost the baby and developed septicaemia. My sister had only been alive for a very short period of time and I never knew her.

My sister's existence re-emerged some years later, when I was again confined to the bedroom during one of my 'summer cold' retreats. In boredom, I began to rummage through some drawers and came across a little child's brush and comb. I asked mother 'what's this?' She reacted hysterically. After she calmed down, she mentioned there had once been another child who had died: my sister. That's the only 'conversation' I've had with her in my entire life about my sister. Like the school inspector story, like being told I was loved, I have had to find the rest from elsewhere.

It feels like a control mechanism she has over me: like she doesn't want me to escape from her grasp.

I'm not sure if I was frightened of her. I had always been told 'whatever you do, don't upset Renee, don't upset your mother'. I can remember my dad saying it, granddad Arthur saying it, Auntie Gwen saying it – and I'm aware of it from other uncles and aunts. If mother began to get hysterical, it would beam into me 'don't upset Renee, don't upset your mother'.

'Don't upset Renee' was based on the view that she'd suffered losing her baby and hadn't been properly cared for afterwards. I think dad's family couldn't understand her. They all loved my dad, so they put up with her behaviour. At the slightest moment, Renee would become upset, and would launch into a tantrum of screaming or crying.

Maybe the times had something to do with it.

In the years after the second world war, people aspired to be the 'nuclear family' – it's also been called the 'Janet and John' syndrome – where the ideal household consisted of heterosexual husband, wife and children, ideally a boy and a girl, living together in blissful interdependence. The picture painted in the 'Janet and John' children's books was of daddy and John gardening outside and mummy and Janet cooking and baking inside. It was the desired lifestyle of its day and I think that's what mother wanted.

But 'Janet' had died. No one, least of all Renee herself, ever addressed this internal turmoil. And to think that mother and dad were together for 60 years.

Mother never had to go out to work to earn any money. She never had an understanding of a working environment. She totally disapproved of any woman who ever went to work. As far as she was concerned, they were third class citizens. Mother did everything to do with running the home. There was only ever one income coming in to the home. That was dad's and it was a struggle for him. I don't know how mother spent her time.

One night, when I was seven or eight and had been sent to bed, I was roused by a disturbance downstairs. I was told I was never supposed to get out of bed, but children are children, and I didn't want to be excluded – I was curious to see what was going on. But I was smaller than the banister rail on the stairs, and I couldn't see over it. So I crept all the way down to the bottom of the stairs. When I got into the hallway, I saw dad with his back to the front door and his hands up in the 'surrender' position. I looked around the foot of the banister rail and there was mother coming down the hall brandishing a carving knife. I can't remember it in any more detail. I imagine she was going to stab him and I prevented it happening because she didn't want me getting in the way. I know I went back to bed. Mother didn't come up to my room but my dad did. It seems strange when I recall what he said to me: 'Don't worry, if your mother ever does that, I'll sell the house'.

Maybe the house had something to do with it.

In those days, my dad shared a very strong principle with my granddad Arthur about maintaining a long line of Nottinghamshire families and about property continuing through the line. It was important to them. The house I lived in with mother and dad was owned outright by dad. Mother's name was never on the deeds. When dad died, the house passed to me.

I remember being told how this manifested itself in another incident years later. It was the late 1960s. By then, I had met my wife Anne and we were joining in the new trend of taking continental holidays to places like Majorca and Ibiza. Anne's mum and dad decided to follow the example and so did mother and dad. At the same time, they decided to make a will 'in case something happened while they were away'. They arranged a meeting with a solicitor and mother outlined what she would like. At this point, dad stood up – for such an outwardly mild man, a statement in itself – and said 'no, no, I don't want that to happen. If that happens, my wife will leave and get married to somebody else and the family money will go out of the family'. Mother has since told me that she hated dad from that moment on.

I had already experienced what this was like for myself. At the age of 13, there was a major defining moment between mother and I. From this point on, it would never be the same between us.

I had misbehaved at school: it was nothing of any significance, but enough for me to be given Saturday detention. When I told my parents that I had to go into school on the Saturday morning, mother simply went very quiet. When I got back from detention, there was a marked difference in her behaviour towards me. I could feel it, almost touch it. She was stand offish, as if she were saying 'get away from me, I can't understand this, you have let me down. You could have tried harder.'

I had upset Renee.

CHAPTER FOUR

School caps, rubbed collars and unfastened blouses

I can remember what I was wearing the day I came back from detention to my cool reception – my grey mac with belt tightened around my waist, school shorts and a school cap. A school cap. At that age.

I didn't get any qualifications at school. The powers–that–be thought it was 'uneconomical' to let me sit maths, because it would have been 'a waste of paper'. But you had to find a job before you left school and it was decided that I would go and work for Uncle Jim.

Jim was a self-made man who had walked down from Scotland in search of work and set up his own upholstery business in Long Eaton. He wasn't a real uncle. He lived next door and was a friend of my dad.

We arranged to visit his factory to finalise all the arrangements on the same day that I was taking part in the annual school sports event. I had been picked to take part in the great mile race. There were to have been eight runners and I had finished ninth in the qualifiers, but the teacher broke with tradition and allowed me to take part. I must have come in about half way down the field, but inside, mentally, it was a victory for me.

Mother and dad were there and I thought they would be pleased, but they never said 'well done' or anything like that.

We left the sports day and dad and I went to see Uncle Jim. We did not receive the greeting we had expected. Jim turned to my dad and said 'Look, I'm awfully sorry about this, but my two sons have decided they don't want Michael to join the business so I'm afraid I can't take him on'. I wasn't upset at all, because I was useless and they would have only ended up sacking me. Jim and dad talked about not falling out, but my dad must have been mortified. Not only because his friend had let him down, but also because we now had to go home and confront mother.

I went and hid. I can remember dad finding it a struggle to get the words out. Well, she wasn't having any of it.

Day after day, the Nottingham Evening Post was produced and mother and dad went through it looking for jobs. Eventually they found me a place called William Dixon's on Hounds Gate, wholesale textile people who also owned the Dixon & Parker school outfitting shops. They were advertising for a trainee salesman and I always remember it said 'parents interest welcomed'. Very unusual and rather quaint. Mother rang up and got an interview. I came home from school one day and was told that, the following night, I would be attending the interview with my dad.

On the night, we were invited into the boardroom to meet the chairman, Sam Small – a charming, very wealthy Jewish businessman. My dad was feeling rather humble. He didn't wear a cloth cap but the occasion felt as if he should have done.

I had my hair brushed back and I was wearing. . . my school uniform. To an interview with a school outfitter.

The offer was made to me of four pounds one shilling a week. Dad was satisfied and it was agreed that I would start the following week. This meant that I missed all of the end–of–school fun. While my fellow pupils were causing mischief in the science lab and chasing all the girls from the neighbouring high school – all the activities I really wanted to be a part of at the age of 16 – I had to start work.

Mother took me to work on my first day. I can remember what I was wearing. My school uniform. Blazer. . . grey trousers. . . but not the cap.

Mother thought the uniform would distinguish me. It did. On my second day, two lads sensed my awkwardness and apprehension and trapped me in a lift shaft to beat me up.

After the third or fourth day I stopped wearing the school uniform and started wearing an old sports jacket, which I'd had since the age of about 12, and a pair of grey flannels.

I didn't have much choice. These were the only clothes I had. Before too much longer, I began to realise why I didn't have any other clothes. It was a trap, it meant mother could retain control over me.

It was a time when fashion was coming in after years of dull, post–war clothing. I'd now got some spending money so I bought a shirt, but it would go missing. I would discover it in a drawer somewhere a week or so later. Mother had hidden it. Without the shirt, I couldn't go out. And I had started to have a girlfriend. I really did like her. We went to places like the cinema and the Goose Fair but mother was very uncomfortable about having her in the house. She could only visit if accompanied by a friend.

I would place shirts in the linen bin to be washed and ironed, because mother did all the housework, and when I was ready to wear them, I would find that the collars had been rubbed raw. So I couldn't go out. I would say: 'What have you done with my shirt?' and she would say 'I haven't done anything'. She would begin to get hysterical and it would beam into me – 'don't upset Renee, don't upset your mother'.

If it were foggy, if I couldn't see Long Eaton gasworks a mile or so away across the fields because of the fog, mother would hide the house keys and refuse to let me out. I didn't know how to argue, how to handle it. Eventually, I climbed out of the window, but it took a lot of assertion on my part.

Mother and dad were never affectionate towards each other. They didn't hold hands. There were no cuddles in the house, no kisses, never any physical connection between the two. I'm sure that, today, people wouldn't stay together under those circumstances: they'd go off and find someone or something else.

One of my last recollections of school days was when 1962 was turning into 1963. It was an incredibly cold winter. Blizzards, ice and and freezing fog. The school heating couldn't take the strain. The headmaster decided it was too cold to stay in the classroom and we were sent home early.

As I walked in the back door at home, I called out 'hello mum'. There was no reply. Then there was an unusual, muffled sound and mother replied 'hello darling, I'll be with you in a minute, I'll be there in a minute.' She appeared at the lounge door and seemed to be a bit flustered, as if she were fastening something around her chest. Then, looming behind her, I saw an extremely familiar figure, with a big grin on his face. I put it out of my mind. I didn't know the first thing about sex and I certainly didn't associate it with mother. But I couldn't believe she had been in there with that particular person.

There was an absolutely devoted, caring side to mother. She cared for 'Buzzy', her stepfather, in his later life. She did everything she could for grandad Arthur, dad's father. When relatives weren't well, she would cook meals for them – she was a wonderful cook – and dad would deliver the meals on a tray. It all satisfied her caring nature.

But she was driven by a belief that, if she looked after people, they would all leave their property to me. She used to talk to me about it. She would say: 'Just think, if we do that for Auntie Dorothy and Uncle Bill, or Uncle Harold, we could get the house.' Of course, houses were never left to us and I think my dad was floored by it.

My family informant, Auntie Gwen, can remember going to mother's house during one of the blackouts in the war and finding mother on the sofa with a soldier called Ted. Dad wasn't there because he'd gone to get some fish and chips. When Gwen discussed this with me, I asked her how she had known that mother had been up to no good. She replied that Renee had seemed flustered and had been noticed fastening up her blouse around her neck. At the end of the war, mother would travel to London on the train every Saturday. Dad thought she was visiting her mum and 'Buzzy'. But she was seeing Ted.

There was also the time that news reached mother that her niece, Anne, had taken up with her married boss at work after divorcing her husband. Mother vowed to do everything she could for Anne's son, Darren. Darren never actually lived in the house but he became a regular part of mother's life. When I wasn't there, he was. In recent years, mother has presented the case that she cared more for Darren than she did for me.

For years and years, mother performed tremendous duties for a neighbour, I'll call him Ben. Ben had been diagnosed as having Downs syndrome. He would visit the house and mother would provide tea and sympathy and play the piano for him. Dad would join in when he was around.

Years later, the last thing to come out of mother's house when she moved into the care home was a picture of Ben's dad, found by the cleaners behind the tiles in the kitchen. Her last flame. All this time, she'd also been seeing Ben's dad.

CHAPTER FIVE

Packhoss

My first job as a 'trainee salesman' at Dixon & Parker was to go down to the yard, unload heavy boxes of men's socks from the delivery lorries, heave all the material into the lift and bring it back upstairs to sort it out.

I worked in a 'half–hose' department. Across the corridor was men's underwear, to the left was ladies' underwear, there were departments for gloves, hats, shirts and – one that really interested me – 'men's fancy', which was ties, cufflinks, armbands, scarves, silks and the like.

But this wasn't to concern me. Once I had sorted through the socks on this floor, I had to make my way upstairs again to a storeroom on the next floor.

This was where all the merchandise for particular seasons or periods of commercial activity was kept. Dixon's used to buy material months in advance for sale times. There were two sales a year, in January and at the end of summer. Business in those days was based on stockholding. It was critical to have a good supply for a long period of time. It guaranteed delivery.

The lift did not go up to the next floor. The only way up was by a narrow set of wooden stairs. I wasn't very strong but I had to lift up the boxes of reorganised goods and wind my way up those stairs. I hated it. Hated it. My head would drop, and my shoulders would stoop and I would take heavy, trudging steps. And I would acquire a nickname that still makes me shudder to this day.

As all the other lads and employers heard me approaching,

they would say: 'Oh, here he comes. Packhoss.'

When I wasn't being 'packhoss', I was still clambering up and down those flights of stairs to fetch cups of tea from the canteen for the men – about 50 in total.

There never was a salesman's job. I was a labourer. What I did revolved around the yard, the stairs, the storeroom and a promise that 'you might become a salesman one day when we get a vacancy'.

I fell into a depressed stupor.

After a couple of years, I was transferred to men's underwear department. I had to break open massive containers that were arriving from China. I couldn't stand it. I was so bloody miserable that, one day, I just burst into tears. It caused a bit of a scene. The next thing I knew, I was whipped off to 'men's fancy'. I was all right there. The department had a younger manager, a bit of a lad about town, and I liked the items they bought and sold. I became more interested.

I had also begun to develop more of a life outside work and home.

It all started with Carolyn Woodhams. One day, at the old Mount Street bus station in Nottingham, I was looking out from my seat on the top deck of a Barton's bus and I spotted her walking along the platform.

I just looked at this girl and I thought 'my god, this is so wonderful'. There was something like electricity.

The next day she and her pals got on the same bus and I can't remember how we got into conversation, but we did, and I couldn't believe it. I had a travelling companion, a very handsome young chap – not a friend, I didn't have any friends – and I think that probably drew them on. I didn't think I was good–looking at all. I thought I was a frump and I behaved like one. But there was something in my character that got going and Carolyn and I started to date.

We went to the Goose Fair and probably went on the dodgems about 43 times, I think – because it meant I could put my arm around her! It was unbelievable. But I hadn't got a clue about sex, not the slightest clue. I'd got a sort of a drive but I didn't understand anything else. It was ages before I even kissed her.

Carolyn used to go to Attenborough Youth Club, so I started to go as well. But it was decreed that I could only go to the youth club, I couldn't go anywhere else, and I had to be home by half past nine. That was a bit of a drag. The youth club didn't finish until ten and I wanted to take Carolyn home. Promisingly, she lived on Shady Lane! But I had to leave the youth club at nine and hurry home.

Eventually, the youth club leaders decided to organise a two-week summer holiday to Ireland. We were to catch a train from Beeston station, change at Crewe, then go on to Holyhead and catch the steamer to Dunleary, where we would stay at a nearby boarding school. By this time, Carolyn had left me for more of a macho type but I signed up for the holiday along with 49 other members. Mother and dad took me to Beeston station to catch the train. There were all these people, some I looked up to, some who looked very strange and sophisticated, the local heroes and heroines, all the characters from Beeston, Attenborough and Chilwell. And there was me, wearing my sports jacket.

Well, we got on the train, and the next day, I had 49 friends. My whole world changed. I became the life and soul of the party. I couldn't believe it myself. If I went anywhere, folks wanted to come with me. I had an absolute ball. That holiday was a marker point and I knew it at the time, because I had thought nobody liked me. I returned from Ireland with a social life.

The two lives of Sylvester.

Back at Dixon & Parker, I had started to run the dressing gown warehouse. This was based in a subterranean grotto that had been an air raid shelter. Both the Pacamac and cloth warehouses were also underneath the building and I began to get on with all the lads who worked in there. They were the same age as me and we had good fun.

I'd shaken off 'packhoss'.

All the gowns came down from the factory on the fifth floor by barrow. I had to sort them out and prepare all the orders. I brought someone in to do the packaging – a bit of initiative on my part. Admittedly, I skived a bit, but when we had to despatch a lot of orders, we did it.

There were racks upon racks of gowns, all coded in numbers and sizes and colours and styles. There's no sound in a room full of cloth. It was dark in there as well. It was peaceful.

Sometimes I would not see a soul all day. One day, though, I heard ponderous, purposeful footsteps approaching. This was highly unusual. They turned out to be the footsteps of the managing director, Bob Morris. I was petrified because all the department managers viewed this shrewd businessman with caution. Why was he paying me a visit without any previous reference through my line manager? I began to shake and wish that I had tried harder at organising the dressing gown warehouse.

He entered the warehouse and sat on a pile of corregated cardboard packing material. He had never spoken to me before. My heart stopped. He began to speak slowly and seriously. "Morning, Michael." I was surprised he knew my name.

He cupped his face in his hands. "I have been thinking. People have more leisure time than ever before and there are new ways of heating our homes being brought in, so they won't need woollen dressing gowns in the future. They will want to wear something different. What shall we design for them that meets their needs instead of dressing gowns, Michael?"

For the first time in my life, someone was taking me seriously and appeared to value my opinion. In his eyes, I knew about the products and saw where they were sent. We spent the morning talking as equals, sharing and solving the same problem. Eventually, we envisaged a lightweight dressing gown made of man made fibres, easy to wear and wash in newly-invented automatic washing machines. Within a few weeks, it had been refined into a shorter type of gown resembling a jacket. It sold brilliantly.

We never thought about trousers, though. Looking back at my first foray into marketing, I realise that if we had pursued this further, we would have had the original concept of a tracksuit. So near and yet so far. . .

Working in the warehouse, I also began to realise that, at the end of certain months, the manager was trying to hit 'a target'. What was this target? It was news to me that we had to sell and complete a set of work against a financial requirement. I wanted to find out more.

These targets were on the wall of the accountant's department and I visited their office to see them. There were actually two targets for dressing gowns, so there must have been two different types of product. This intrigued me. I started to get all the orders and I worked like mad, then I'd go back to the accountant's department to see if we'd exceeded the target. Nobody ever said 'well done' but I found it interesting and I began to do it every week. We always got over the target. That's been with me ever since. Target–orientated.

Another financial responsibility loomed large at this time. I had met my wife–to–be Anne. I was 19. Anne was 16 and still at school. She hadn't got any earnings. I wanted to be with her and to take her out. Anne's grandma had an old saying. It came home to roost. This was the moment in life when 'a penny bun costs tuppence'.

I decided that I needed more money, so I left Dixon & Parker and went to work in the office of Guy Birkins, a lace factory in Bakersfield, for an increase of 50p a week. In the mornings, I would catch the bus into Nottingham from my home in Toton, then another in to Bakersfield. At the end of the working day, I would catch the two buses home again and then, in the evening, I was in the bus queues again to go and see Anne in Eastwood.

On one occasion, I knocked on the back door at Anne's house and her dad, Ken, answered: "Hello Michael, Anne's not here, she's gone to an organ recital at church with her mum and grandma." I thought, 'of course, that's what you do' and suggested that I'd better go again. "No, no," Ken said. "Come on in, nice to see you, how are you? I tell you what, why don't we go down to the Sun Inn in Eastwood? We can go into the Engine Room and have a pint."

I couldn't believe it. I was going from my dad, who didn't drink, to this bloke who actually wanted to take me for a pint. I was up for that.

We jumped into his car and called in at the hotel. He seemed to know everybody in there. He was fabulous, he bought me a pint and talked to me like a contemporary, we began a really good conversation. Then the pub door opened and a huge man came over and joined us. Ken introduced him. "Michael, this is Anne's cousin, John." I learned that he was a miner, and he took up a position on the other side of me. "Nice to meet you," John said, and asked me if I'd like another drink. After a couple more pints, the door opened again, and a wild-looking individual stood behind me. I thought, 'what have we got here?' It turned out to be Uncle Frank, a pick and shovel man, hard as nails. Originally from Doncaster, he had become pit deputy at Eastwood. It became clear that he wasn't a man to be argued with. I was unnerved. It also began to dawn upon me that the three of them were doing this by design. They were vetting me. Between them, they found out everything about me. I passed the test.

Ken was very kind. You could sit down and talk to him. He'd give you a hug. He would become one of my best friends very quickly. And Anne's mum, Nancy, was lovely. I don't know how she ever tolerated my mother. Like me, Anne was an only child. Nancy took to me like a son, but mother never took to Anne. Perhaps it was because she had an issue about daughters.

Ken would regularly give me lifts home from their house in his car. Both he and my dad eventually taught me how to drive and I gained my licence. Dad never said 'well done' or anything like that. I think he was pleased inwardly. I thought that, if I could get transport, then I would be able to see Anne more often and we would have freedom. But I still had the problems of no savings and a low wage.

I noticed that there were people called commercial travellers who had company cars, and so that's what I decided to be. Ken had recognised that I had some talent and he knew I wasn't happy at the lace factory. He came across an advert in the paper for a junior retail salesperson at a leading food brand company. I filled in the application. When it came to the interview, Ken met me from work and took me to the hotel where the interviews were being held. He even brought a suit for me to wear. But there were two candidates for one job and I wasn't the one chosen.

However, two weeks later, the company rang up and said 'if you'd like to join us and learn about the grocery trade and selling, we're going to create two jobs'. I was offered double my wages and a Morris 1000 Traveller car.

It was freedom at last. I started the following Monday.

CHAPTER SIX

Bully for Michael

Mother and dad were on holiday when I got the job with the food company. I announced the 'fait accomplis' on their return.

Mother was disgusted. I hadn't got a job in a bank with a desk of my own. Her mood lifted when she realised I was now wearing a suit and I would be able to pull up outside the house in my own car – more for the satisfaction it would accrue from prying neighbours, I suspect, than on her own behalf. Dad never said anything. I think he would have been astounded. I was as well, because I had shown some initiative and exerted a little influence. A major company in fast moving consumer goods, a brand leader based overseas, had created two jobs and got back to me. It was exciting. I had really wanted it and I had got it.

It was like starting out on my own terms rather than being conditioned – a conditioning I had never understood.

My job description was retail sales rep and my products were tinned hams and foodstuffs. I drove my Morris 1000 into Lincolnshire and Derbyshire on sales trips and, on other occasions, I travelled further afield and even stayed away from home. I would be told which customers to go and visit by Harry Selby, the branch manager. These were mainly small shops and buying groups. He took responsibility for all the big cash and carry outlets and wholesalers.

One day, he said: 'Michael, I'd like you to call on the Co–op. I've got permission from the grocery buyer for you to visit all the branches and introduce our range of products to all the managers. Bring all the orders back to me. I'll collate them and I'll tell the buyer what you've sold and he'll do his ordering and distribution through us.'

Well, my dad worked for the Co–op. It had 30 branches.

I told him of the opportunity I'd been given and asked him if he had any ideas on how I could go about it. He said: 'You'll remember a lot of these managers from watching me play cricket with them when you were a little lad. I'll pass the word around that you're coming, so they will make you welcome. If there's anyone you don't recognise, just say hello, I'm Michael Sylvester, do you know my dad Les? They'll make sure you're all right'.

It took me a week to go around all the shops in the outlying villages. But the managers bought like crazy. I can't remember how many cases, but it was hundreds. I reported back to Harry Selby and he nearly fell off his chair. I'd done well but I didn't know how well. The previous rep had gone round and sold 25 cases. I got permission to conduct the round every couple of months, and then I was given a list of supermarkets in another area.

I began to shed all the fears from the past and to think 'I can do this.'

But while my eyes were being opened as promised to grocery and selling, there were elements of the experience that I already understood only too well. It took me back to the village primary school and to being chased home at the end of classes, to memories of just getting inside the gate before my pursuers could catch me, of them standing outside my home and waiting for me to come out again. I can't remember blows ever being landed, but they would push me about and there were daily threats.

My exciting new marketplace had a lot to do with bullying.

This was highlighted by a new retail development of moving products from behind a counter into open display and encouraging people to choose the goods themselves – the onset of supermarkets.

The people behind this concept in the Nottingham area bought a building but were unable to afford fixtures or fittings or to pay any staff. Salesmen from the food companies were therefore 'invited' to stock the buildings themselves with their own products. On a Sunday morning, I would be among 60 representatives of grocery companies lined up inside the supermarket building. It was like a starting line. We were waiting for the manager to blow a whistle. When he did, we had to run into the warehouse, collect a box of our produce, run back out, cut open the cases and stack them on to the pallets. My cases contained 1lb hams, 48 in all. I couldn't shift them quickly enough, but I managed to secure a couple of rows.

That's how the shelves were stocked and the shop was laid out. There was no accountability for people's fitness, age or condition of health. If you didn't run quickly, you didn't get the floor space. If you didn't get the floor space, you couldn't sell your products. If you couldn't sell your products, you wouldn't get any more orders from the supermarket.

Before long, the bullying assumed other guises. We were asked to drop prices where we could. Then it became 'if you don't give us some free samples, we won't give you an order'. Or 'if you keep it quiet that this stock was damaged, you'll get a credit'. Or 'if you don't do this or the other, we'll ring up your national sales manager and get you the sack'. There was something different all the time. It was bullying and it was manipulation.

Other distasteful examples emerged as supermarkets strove to gain a hold. One supermarket company would make its profit by selling products to its store managers at retail price, rather than wholesale, therefore forcing the managers to come up with other ways to make their own profits. One tactic they used to achieve this was 'buncing' – the appearance that savings were being made on special offers, whereas, on close inspection, the price was actually being increased. Another was for checkout operatives to 'ring up' extra items as they went through. Nobody noticed because customers had been waiting in a queue and simply wanted to get out of the shop and go home: they were not in the habit of checking. I'm not saying this happens now, but that was merchandising in those days.

After three years, I moved to a larger company in fast-moving consumer goods, one of the companies to aspire to if you were a rep. A satisfying consequence of this move, not the main motivation, was more power over the bullies. As just another supplier of tinned meat, my previous employers could be pushed around and bargained with. As an enormous brand leader of essentials – such as salt, pepper and flour – my new employers couldn't. More importantly in personal terms, I progressed to learning about planned selling and discipline.

I became a specialist in managing a sales territory using a methodical and numerical approach. It was quite different for me because it wasn't about character or influence, it was about systems and being task–driven. Computers were being introduced, but these were strictly office–based. I invented an 'in car' method of administration. I made a number of calls a day in a certain journey order and, at the end of the day, sent a postcard to the people I'd be visiting the following week. I also did time and motion studies. It was held up as an example to others and they would request to see it in action.

Eventually, the supermarkets began to find a way of bullying the bigger companies and my employers moved into more of a bullying culture itself. Firms were merged and we got a boss from one of the other divisions who simply made people feel frightened.

Anne and I were now married and I wanted to get out of the grocery trade, so I went into cosmetics as a sales trainer. This time the main company was based in Germany, UK operations were run out of Aylesbury, and I worked from my new married home.

I would go to places like colleges, sell–in stock for the hairdressing school and take along a professional hairdresser from London who would teach the students for a short period and put them through a qualification. I would also teach the students about how to stock a retail shop. We were building new markets as the students joined the adult and business worlds and I thought, 'I like this'.

But frustration set in when I perceived that I couldn't become a manager.

Retailing was changing and I wanted to be in the frontline. I joined an electrical spares manufacturer as a sales representative. It was at the time of the marketing innovation of blister packs. My company provided every type of spare imaginable to retailers and electricians through wholesalers. Shops would order, say, a box of 100 plug tops. Each plug top was in a blister pack on a card, branded, and with the price printed on it. All the retailer had to do was to display the packs on a stand. It took away all their worries about charging at the right price: they were guaranteed a profit.

My company had an established sales force behind this introduction. I joined it, bringing my planned selling methods with me. I opened up Co–op stores to the products. This gave me display stands in 20 stores with payments on commission. My volume increased. It was a company that valued its people. I hadn't come across this before and it felt good. I got on well with the people who were there and I continued to do very well for a number of years – until that nagging feeling struck again. I felt that I should be moving up to become a manager. I made several approaches about a promotion. I couldn't understand the fact they didn't have any vacancies for a manager. I thought that they should have created one.

I saw a vacancy with a dishwasher company for an area manager for the East Midlands. I thought, 'that is what I want'. I had a vision in my mind of what it would be like to be area manager. These were men who commanded substantial sales teams and managed key accounts. The company took one look at the experience I had got and moved rapidly to appoint me. I took up my post and it became apparent just as rapidly that I was on my own. There was supposed to have been a merchandising team but it had dispensed with in order to finance my appointment.

I was charged with selling dishwashers, washing machines and other white goods. I felt it called for sharp practices – which was not me, and never had been. I realised that the odds were against me doing it on my own. Every store I visited had already got washing machines and Hoovers and Hotpoints, so they weren't interested. And dishwashers were seen as an unwelcome American influence – *'we wash the pots by hand, m'duck, that's what you're supposed to do'* – so I set about trying to educate people in the 'new way'. I persuaded stores to take on limited stock, with the proviso that I would pay for someone to act as a salesperson in the store at peak shopping times. That way, the store would have a staffed 'white goods department'. Hoover and other companies also employed demonstrators for their goods. The stores liked it because it looked as though they had showrooms full of staff. It was good for us because we had people on the spot to attract customers towards our products and to explain the benefits to them. It was quite competitive but I ended up with a staff of about ten. We also developed a service side, run by somebody else.

But it was hard to sell enough to make it pay, and I got the feeling that the management of the company started to turn against me. Selling requires emotion and people become vulnerable. I perceived that I had become regarded as the weak link, that the lack of sales was my fault. Anne had just given birth to our first son, James, and I can remember going to register the birth in Nottingham carrying the fear that, in a few days' time, I would be out of a job.

I should have placed my behaviour in context, accepted that the relationship was not going to work, maintained good relations with everybody and taken my time to find another job. But I didn't. My boss picked up on some aspects of my behaviour at a seminar with a group of buyers and I reacted badly. I acted as if I were being bullied and we had a fall–out.

I saw a vacancy for a Midlands sales representative at a hosiery manufacturer in Leicester. I liked clothes, the touch and feel of the textures and products, and it was an interesting time in marketing. I applied, but I still regarded it as a 'demotion'.

To me, even though it hadn't turned out as expected, I had been 'the manager'.

CHAPTER SEVEN

Life of a salesman

I learned a lot at the hosiery company. We stocked wide varieties of socks and hosiery and created two ranges a year. It was my job to go to all the major stores – Harrods, House of Fraser, Rackhams, John Lewis – and interest them in buying from one range before introducing the next. I used the systematic side that I'd picked up years before and measured my business in each account as I went along. I set myself targets to try and beat. I started increasing my territory.

I always approached customers with a new story – 'I've got a new range', 'I've got a new product' or 'there's something you need to be aware of'. I started to talk to them about wider developments in the marketplace, in fashion and in related business. I presented them with information before I presented the range. They found it interesting and they looked out for me. It was successful and I felt I was a good salesperson.

We used to take the annual 'Knitters Fortnight' holidays at the beginning of July and Anne and I were preparing to take our break one Friday night when she drew my attention to an item on the Midlands television news. A fire had broken out at one of Leicester's main factories. It turned out to be one of the factories owned by my company – a rambling, five–storey Victorian structure. It was an enormous blaze. No–one was injured. All the workers in the factory had left for their holidays. But my first reaction was 'I've lost my job. No socks, nothing to sell'. At 7.30am the following day, I stood outside the factory gates in Leicester staring at the collapsed remains. The fire brigade was mopping up and there were a few directors about.

I didn't know what to do. A second building, where all the administration was carried out, had been saved. In a state of shock, I wandered into it. One of the directors saw the anxiety on my face. He took me to one side and told me: 'Michael, you must not worry about a thing. We have a plan'.

Builders were to clear the factory and erect Portakabins in its place. Production was to be moved to an out–of–town site in Aylestone, and we were to move there as well. It was a single-storey disused building with concrete floor, missing windows and weeds in the guttering. But services were still there. At least we could make a start. The director told me to continue looking after our customers and to reassure them that we would remain in business.

I became a member of a hastily–arranged team attempting to create order from the chaos. We negotiated with the insurance company and settled on 80% of the claim. It was paid out within a matter of weeks. My company – which had previously operated a strict policy of purchasing rather than taking out hire purchase arrangements or loans – also opened up dialogue with the banks. So it simultaneously became cash rich and had access to loan facilities if necessary.

I contacted suppliers and told them we intended to be back in business quickly. However, we could not honour all the commitments we had previously made, so I asked them to hold goods with us and we would draw it off over a period of time. I made a point of mentioning that we would remember those who had looked after us. This helped to ensure that, for the meantime, we would be protected from any price increases.

At the same time, customers were worried about supplies of stocks for the back–to–school period. We drew up an allocation system to guarantee each customer as fair a supply as we could under the circumstances and made appointments with them all to explain it. The directors also negotiated new terms with major customers like Marks & Spencer and Mothercare and we were able to develop new lines in children's fashion from our out–of–town site.

All this activity laid the foundations for a major turn–around in fortunes and it was a significant experience for two reasons. First, it would give me the basis for an effective role–play training exercise that I would introduce in another environment years later. Secondly, and more crucially for the time being, I believe it was the moment that the director earmarked me for the role I had coveted.

When we returned to the road as salesman, we had to go and collect our stock from a warehouse in the centre of the city. One day, I called in at the warehouse and discovered that the manager had left. Before the end of the day, the moment I had been waiting for actually arrived. The director installed me as temporary replacement manager – and this time, the position did match up to my vision.

I had responsibility for 47 staff working in a three–storey building, full of stock. It was truly what I had wanted and what my dad had wanted for me. I was in my element and I gave it everything I had got.

I organised a record stocktaking in two days. Previously, for this to take place, the business had been closed down for a week. I developed a review of which parcel carriers we used, which could have potentially saved the company £30,000 a year in transport costs. And I set up regular meetings with the two factory managers.

Every Friday lunchtime, I would have fish and chips with them in the main factory. It was totally informal and inspirational. One of us would buy the fish and chips from a local shop and we would then sit in an office with our feet up on the desk. There was no pressure. I could find out what was happening inside the factory and all sorts of conversations and ideas would come up.

There was one occasion when we took delivery of a new German hi-tech knitting machine for a pilot run. I can't remember the number of needles it had: it was unlike any machine we had seen before. One Friday, we had all gathered around with our fish and chips and I asked 'how long can it run?' Both managers said 'we don't know'. So one of them fetched a cone of red yarn, the only piece of yarn to hand, and placed it on the spook. We set the machine running. When the spindle came to the end and the machine tidied up the hose, we had a contender for the biggest sock in the world. We all had a laugh about it. We also had a great marketing opportunity. I sold them for £5 each to all the department stores as Father Christmas stockings. It made extra income and used up all the old yarn.

One day, my secretary buzzed through and said 'there's a gentleman sitting in reception. The director has sent him and wants you take him on a tour around the warehouse'. I thought he must have been an influential customer so I showed him everything – how storage worked, how the trucking distribution worked, how the whole system worked. When we got back to my office, I made him a cup of tea and asked: 'so why have you been asked to come and have a look around the warehouse?' 'Oh', he replied, 'I'm going to be the new warehouse manager'.

Within 20 minutes of my guest leaving, I charged round to head office, barged through the director's door and unleashed a verbal volley. He seemed very calm. He asked me to sit down and have a cup of coffee. He was smoking a big cigar and, in between each draw, he repeated: 'Michael, Michael, why are you here?' Eventually he explained: 'you're here because I sent for you, I just wanted to see if you really wanted that job or not'.

The position was never confirmed on a permanent basis. I never found out why, perhaps it was office politics. On my birthday that year, I received a letter from the company. 'Thank you for your time as manager, we'd now like you to go back to the sales department'. I couldn't handle it, I felt totally rejected. My heart was lost. I left within three months.

I returned to the electrical spares manufacturer as a district manager. I had maintained a good relationship with them even though some years had passed and new people had taken over the top positions. One of the newcomers was sales and marketing director, John Parker. I really admired John. He was ahead of his time, one of the first new businessmen to embrace equality. He changed my business life. He saw potential in me and sent to me to Ashridge Management College. It opened me up to so much. I was promoted from area manager to regional manager, with responsibility for a salesforce between the Mersey and the Thames.

One day he called all regional managers to a meeting. He sat informally in front of us and said 'gentleman, I need to explain to you that the company has sold out to a millionaire, effective from this morning. You will have a new chairman, a new managing director, and there will be a new way of working from now on. I've decided not to stay with the group, I have taken another job elsewhere, so I think it's best I just leave the room'.

And as my inspiration left, an uncouth young chap entered. I looked in horror at the dignified person who had left, and the opposite who had come in. I tried to get on with it but I started to deteriorate in my work.

I returned to the 'situations vacant' columns.

CHAPTER EIGHT

Letdown

By now, it was the mid 1980s, and I had become fascinated by logistics and distribution. An opportunity arose for me to make my mark with a Midlands–based parcel carrier.

It was a family–owned firm, very old–fashioned in many ways, with a quality product but a falling customer base. The board were enthusiastic for somebody with a new way of thinking, who understood fast moving consumer goods, who knew about marketing and who could lead their business into the era of international distribution in the face of increasingly ruthless competition from overseas.

I had emerged freshly inspired from my time at Ashridge Management College. It had opened up a whole new world of marketing to me. I developed an insatiable appetite for learning about new processes. I became a member of the National Institute of Physical Distribution and Logistics and I set myself for the challenge.

The company had reached the point where it was extremely well known and had a very good reputation but it needed to grow because of aggressive competition.

On my first day in this new battleground, I collected my executive car, expense account and met senior colleagues and customers.

On the second day, I began to realise the job was not quite as it had been presented.

The Scottish office had a major financial deficit, the Welsh office was troubled by restrictive practice, the major London customers were on the verge of a mass exodus and the local salesman had walked off the job.

The chairman was on long–term sick leave in Majorca fighting a life–threatening disease.

And, in my 'office', my predecessor was still behind the desk with absolutely no knowledge of his impending departure.

I drew up a six–point list of priorities to galvanise the business. It included contacting the customer base, familiarising myself with the product, writing a new marketing plan, creating a new sales and marketing team and evaluating the impact of the new dominant overseas forces on the UK market.

These were the heydays of linear thinking and, with hindsight, I need not have given myself so much hard work. By concentrating on just one of my priorities – to communicate with staff, listen to their stories and identify their potential – I would have realised that all the information was already there and all I had to do as a leader was to empower them to get on with the job.

But I had learned that management was all about drive and action – setting targets, raising the profile and the pace, leading from the front, high energy, working hard, setting examples, motivation, identifying who was up for the fight, recruiting new staff, achieving results, instigating change, re–engineering, re–organising and gaining market share and more profit.

And that's what I did. I travelled by air, rail and road to all points of the nation, opening new depots, buying new vehicles and attracting new customers. We doubled the volume, increased the profit, gained market share and gave the company new prestige.

I never saw my family from one day to the next.

Then the chairman returned with a new wife, a new lifestyle

and a new agenda for the future – based around his graduate son taking control.

In the previous two–and–a–half years, I had fallen in love with a product and disregarded the internal politics that exist in a head office. I'd always regarded it as a waste of energy and, in any case, I had not had the time.

Over the next 18 months, as my love affair with the product continued – through more meetings with customers, discussions with staff and development of systems – a boardroom battle got underway.

One Friday afternoon, I was summoned to a board meeting that I had not been told was taking place. I had no sooner entered the boardroom than the chairman informed me I had failed to make enough profit to satisfy the board. He said he didn't want it to be a shock but we were parting company. He asked for the keys to my office and my company car – and my immediate departure. At the same time, icily, he passed on his best wishes to my family.

I waited for the bus to take me on the hour's journey home to no income, a mortgage, a used–up overdraft, credit cards – and a lovely wife and two small children, whom I felt I had let down.

CHAPTER NINE

The odd number

There's a true story I tell in workshops and discussion groups to demonstrate why, at critical moments in our lives, we must acknowledge and process our emotions before we can progress to any logical or meaningful way ahead.

The story is this. . .

It was a beautiful clear August morning when Anne and I, together with our two sons James and Julian, set off on the long–awaited annual family migration to Spain. A chance to leave behind the rigours of work and school.

The taxi driver dropped us off at Birmingham Airport with plenty of time to spare. We could buy a newspaper, coffee and breakfast before our scheduled flight to Malaga.

Our flight was called and we boarded the plane. James and Julian took the window seats and Anne and I took the aisle seats across from each other. The aircraft taxied down the runway and took off to the south, through hazy cloud into wide clear blue skies. When we reached a height of 36,000 feet, the captain introduced himself and predicted clear weather, a straightforward journey and invited us to relax and enjoy the flight. I settled down to read my book.

After about three–quarters of an hour, I noticed that the sun was travelling across the pages of my book – first from the east, then slowly round from the south–east and then from the west. This happened over a period of about five minutes, yet I had not been aware of any change in altitude or the angle of flight. We had not banked or turned.

I spotted the purser walking along the gangway towards the captain's cabin. He was glancing through the portholes from side to side and had an uneasy manner about him.

Moments later, our captain announced that the aircraft was unable to continue the journey to Malaga and we would be returning to Birmingham in an estimated time of 25 minutes. This was because of 'a small technical problem'. There was 'no cause for alarm'.

Along with the rest of the passengers, I thought: 'ok, well there'll be a delay, more waiting, nobody ever tells you what the small technical problem is.' I returned to my book.

We embarked on a slow descent, turning in very wide circles. An hour later, we still had not been asked to prepare to land, and concern began to reappear and spread. Eventually, the captain announced that we had been given clearance. Again, he asked us not to be alarmed – this time, by the sight below of blue flashing lights. The airport had been closed to all other traffic to allow the emergency services to fully mobilise both along the runway and outside the airfield perimeter.

He told us to expect a bumpy landing and a lot of noise. It wasn't said at the time, obviously, but in fact we had been shedding fuel and none of the aircraft flaps were working properly.

It wasn't a particularly bumpy landing but, once back on the ground, it seemed like the plane was never going to stop. The roar of the reverse thrust of the engines was deafening.

The aircraft shuddered to a halt at the end of the runway next to a fire engine and an ambulance. There was complete silence as we taxied to the terminal building, where we disembarked, gathered ourselves and waited to hear of the next development. Within half an hour, a new plane had been provided and we took to the skies again. A familiar voice greeted us with the in–flight details. The same captain was in charge.

Two hours later, after we had arrived safely at Malaga, I sought out the captain and thanked him for his skill and composure under the most trying and dangerous circumstances. He simply said that he been trained for these eventualities and had been through the experience so many times in a 30–year career with both the RAF and the airlines, that his reaction had come as second nature.

Later that evening, as we treated ourselves to a large glass of wine on the balcony of our holiday apartment, Julian turned to me and whispered: "I can't believe that happened Dad – did that actually happen? "

I replied: "Yes, son, it really happened. And to prove it, every time you set out on a journey by air for the rest of your life, you will be returning on an odd number!"

I tell this story to encourage people to relate to what happens when we're faced by challenge. After reading a section of the story, I will refer to a series of questions – such as 'what would have been your reaction to being told there was a problem'? 'What would you have done next?' 'How would you have felt?' 'What would you have thought?'

Of all the thousands of people who have heard this story, many appear to relate to the same things. On hearing that there is a problem with the plane, they will say their thoughts turn to 'how do we get out?' 'What do we take with us?'

On this flight, I can remember that there were some older passengers between me and the emergency door, and I was extremely conscious that I would go over them, or through them if necessary, to get my family to safety. It's horrible the things we will do for self–preservation.

My youngest son Julian's preoccupation was with what we

should take with us if we had to get off the plane quickly. We agreed on passports and credit cards. That's all. Put them in our pockets, carry nothing else and just get out!

Anne's concern was over her difficulty to move quickly because of a recent broken bone in her right foot. She was also worried about being able to carry her handbag. My eldest son James pointed out: "Mum, if we get off this thing, I'll carry your handbag. If we don't, you won't need it anyway. . ."

At this stage of the flight, there was pandemonium among the passengers. Some were crying and starting to scream.

When the story moves on to getting back to the airport terminal, I will ask people – 'what would you have done now', 'how would you have felt'. They all say the same things. 'We would want to talk to somebody, hold somebody'.

They will say that they have had a big shock. They would want to go to the toilet, or smoke, or have a cup of coffee or something stronger, and to talk to other people, even touch other people. They would want to have a cry or a laugh – simply, they would just want to communicate.

They say that, among the last things they would want to be told is that there was another plane waiting for them. They will have had a bad experience and they would want time to recover.

So I will relate this to a workplace situation.

You've had a phone call from a customer, who has been frustrated and abusive to you. At the end of that call, do you want to pick up the phone again? You don't. Even if it's a call centre, where you are being monitored and will be criticised for affecting the number of incoming calls on the board, you don't want to do it. What you actually want to do is to go outside on the step and have a cigarette, or tell your mate about it, or have a cup of tea. Then you've processed it and you can get back on with your work.

If you get back on the phones again, in all likelihood there would be a delayed reaction. You will not only handle the next call badly, but the next two or three down the line, because you've still got this remembered pain and you are de–motivated.

Above all, I have noticed that, when I ask 'what would you be thinking at this point', people will tell me what they feel. When I ask them, 'how would you feel about this', people will tell me what they think.

I believe that feelings overpower thinking and we have to go through feelings before we can find the logic. Often there's confusion in us when we're trying to be logical. We're not accepting it. Our feelings of self–protection are in the way. I try to lead people forward and say 'accept these feelings, understand them, then you can think more clearly'.

CHAPTER TEN

The curse of 'getting there'

Failure. What would the neighbours think? What would my parents think? Their 37–year–old son had got the sack. I felt all the guilt, misery and helplessness of my childhood return.

With the help of ACAS and a firm of industrial solicitors, we obtained Queen's Counsel to help negotiate the best severance deal.

While we were advised that we had a strong case to go to court, we felt unlikely to win more than the compensation already on the table. And there was the potential cost of time and emotional energy to take into account. Bad mouthing, the impact on future references, the effect on my image in the marketplace.

We settled out of court and Anne and I took the children for a holiday in Spain to recover as a family unit.

As the exhaustion from the experience dissipated, I began to see myself again as a desirable commodity. I reckoned that, if I concentrated on career improvement, I could gain a new post in senior management within weeks.

On my return from Spain, my self–esteem was buoyed and I was ready for the challenge. I attended interview after interview after interview. For a whole variety of reasons, none of them came off.

As each day and week went by, I felt hammer blows to my confidence and commitment. We had no money, a repossession letter from the building society and a bank request for overdraft payment,

Anne, however, seemed able to set aside her deep concerns and to offer enormous support. She made do on low cost shopping with my unemployment benefit and rolled up her sleeves. She even made her own bread and pasta to just keep us going. It was at this time I learned that Anne is the A in Activist: a specialist in multi-tasking. I remember on one occasion I asked her to do something and the reply came: 'Yes – and I'll stick a broom handle up my arse and sweep the floor at the same time!" Her true light shone through as it always has – loving, reliable, kind, warm and caring. Intelligent, wise, experienced. Energetic, funny, adorable.

The children must have picked up worried messages from our conversations and behaviour, but they didn't give the appearance of suffering.

Just before Christmas, after I had been unemployed for around six months, I went for an interview with a dairy company in the next village to become a milkman. I simply wanted a job to enable me to feed my family for Christmas and buy presents for our children. It turned into a ritual humiliation.

What was I doing there dressed in a suit? A so–called company director. . . had I been to prison? What had I stolen? Would I run off with the takings? Could I work hard enough? Was I a trouble maker? How could I cope with the pressure of hard work?

The next night, after this belittling and patronising rejection, we attended a charity event in the village. It was for 'old folk and families on hard times'. Taking pride of place at the head of table as 'guest of honour', unbelievably, was my accuser.

As it turned out, there were presents for the children and food on the table at Christmas – thanks to our family and friends, who all gave knowing full well that we had no means of giving anything in return.

After New Year's Day, the long darkness of winter took over. Like a lost explorer beginning to realise that long–awaited rescue was not going to come, despair set in. Well–meaning people said 'don't' worry'. But in that situation, the worry becomes all–consuming.

"When visiting the village shop, I overheard a little girl say 'isn't it a shame what happened to Mr Sylvester?"

"Today Anne found me standing, staring at the toothpaste counter in a local supermarket. I had no idea where I was; I must have been there half an hour."

"At teatime today I burst into tears in front of the children. It must have been an awful experience for them but I simply could not control myself."

"I walked round the village to collect my eldest son James from primary school. I felt everyone was looking at me and I withdrew from the crowd. When James came out of school, he took my hand to take him home and offered to chop up the toy wooden castle I had made for him. 'Then you could use it for firewood, daddy, that would save some money.' The following afternoon he crayoned a picture and hung it up in the front window for all passers by to see. It read 'Toys for sale 5p, 10p and 20p to help dad.'"

These are extracts from a diary I kept at the time. I also turned to the Old Testament book of Job, who had everything taken away and more before it returned thrice fold. Then I studied Proverbs.

I managed to get some work that paid just a few pounds. A local farmer needed a new drive laying for his tractor. It involved carrying heavy barrows of stone along a roadway.

Oh, here he comes. Packhoss.

As I trudged up and down, people driving past would sound the

Illustration by Dominique Smart, smart:man creative, Nottingham

horns and wave to me: people from the village where my family and I had lived for many years. I would bow my head and look away. I could not feed my own family and I felt ashamed.

A friend said to me: "Why do you turn away? We are your friends. It makes no difference to us whether you have money or a company car."

For probably the first time in my life, I began to see that there is more to have and to hold than materialistic might. And I remembered the sailor's adage that the biggest danger when lost at sea is the actual fear of being lost.

I spent more time in the garden, walking in the fields around my home and by the waterside. My mind was freed up from enough fear to allow creativity. I was able to see the whole picture of my life and surroundings.

I had a growing awareneess that the answers lay in getting out of 'could try harder' vertical thinking – the curse of believing that 'getting there' was all about consuming more and trying to get other people to consume more.

This process is referred to as 'right brain thinking' – establishing a feeling of calm and stability within one's self, if only for a short time. Inevitably, it develops self esteem. The 'right brain' absorbs information, works out mechanics, processes information, analyses facts. So at times of difficulty, stress or trauma, it begins to race away at twice the speed. In management we call it managing by crisis. I've noticed it in sales management. Panic sets in and it produces high burn–out rates. The 'left brain' publishes the creative side and usually holds the answers – if only we would take the time to listen.

I was thinking that my greatest business asset lay in the varied fields of European management I had experienced before my 'downfall' – team leader, supervisor, key account manager, trainer, area manager, regional manager, national manager.

Then Anne blasted open a pathway to the 'left brain' with the simplest of questions: "What part of my work experience had I enjoyed most?"

Until that moment, I had solely concentrated on what skills base I had that would produce the most success, or make the most money in the shortest time.

My 'left brain' took over. At first, the answers appeared to be negative. It wasn't supervising, managing or controlling – whether budgets or strategies or markets. It wasn't making profit or hiring and firing or co–ordinating logistics. It wasn't selling or presenting or buying best or chairing meetings. What gave me most satisfaction, if not a thrill, was my skill as a trainer and developer, coach and mentor.

There is no greater buzz than working with another human being from whatever culture or walk of life and helping them to do better for themselves.

Anne and I set about starting a small firm devoted to the training and development of people in the workplace. We had no equipment, office or even a dependable car. I had no experience of self employment. As the parents of two children, we lacked any financial back–up – and with my track record, no investor would be even the slightest bit interested. I did not even have an idea of a company logo or a customer.

I did have a close family and friends and a lot of business acquaintances who could give me advice. I felt fit and healthy. I decided the odds were in my favour.

I found out about a Government scheme to help long–term unemployed people get off benefit and start their own small businesses. There was a pilot course running at a college 30 miles from my home. Applicants had to meet a 'criteria of desperation' before being invited to interview but I was pleased to see that the programme would be run by professional business women and men who had gone through it all themselves. There was a genuine chance of receiving non–patronising practical guidance and support.

The idea behind the programme was to help formulate a business plan and, on the successful completion of five small tests, to provide a small financial grant to help pay tax out of profit at the end of the first period, so freeing up innovation.

My shock came at the end of my interview when the panel – a friendly middle–aged man with a female civil servant assistant – said: "We are sorry Mr Sylvester but we cannot offer you a place on the programme. You are over–qualified."

Their reasoning was that the subject matter and pace of the work would be too slow for me and I would get bored and quit the programme, preventing more deserving people gaining benefit.

I heard a voice well up inside of me. "But I'm desperate. I've never pleaded with anyone in my life before, but I need this help. Please, please."

I raised myself onto very unsteady legs to leave. Then I heard the chairman say: "Wait. If you're prepared to have a go, then so am I."

His assistant said she would partner me with a younger delegate who had been unable to work for six years. He also had a partner and two small children and wanted to start a gardening business. The course would start in two weeks' time.

Two days before the breakthrough day, I received a telephone call. It was from an office supplies company, with which I had been for an interview some weeks before. It was what I had been striving and struggling to find for so many months. They invited me to head up their Midlands sales operation. The position carried a salary matching the package I had previously commanded and a company car. It offered the chance to manage and co–ordinate a huge team of people, control budgets and develop both a new marketing strategy and new business.

"Thank you for the invitation," I replied. "But I will call you back in three weeks time when I've decided whether or not to start a new business."

The telephone went quiet.

CHAPTER ELEVEN

The 'divine leap'

According to the calculations I carried out on the enterprise course, my new business could survive its first year and produce a small profit. But when I progressed to completing the cash flow forecast, a different picture emerged. I would go bust within three months because I would not receive payment quickly enough. We simply lacked the finance to make a start and I did not have a clue how to overcome the stumbling block. Crestfallen, I picked up the phone again to the company that had offered me the job three weeks previously.

And the thought crossed my mind: "What would my mother say if she knew what a fool I had made of myself?"

To my surprise, the company had left open the position and offered me the job. I would be back on the career ladder with a salary to take care of my financial commitments. But having tasted the excitement and having seen the potential of starting my own business, there was also an element of reluctance on my part. My innermost thought was 'I want to leave the management treadmill and follow my new-found ambitions. Helping people to learn is right for me.'

A friend I had met at a village hall dance contacted me and told me he had a client – a high-profile graphic design company – which had asked him for help with management training. My friend had heard of my proposed business venture and wondered if I would be interested in providing that help. It aggravated my dilemma.

I had been tantalised by the possibilities of starting my own business. At the same time I had just endured the tortures of many months out of work. On the one hand, I wanted to use the experience of my course, to have the courage of my convictions. On the other, I was haunted by the risk of it ending in failure and finding myself back in the employment wastelands. While I felt that my time on the corporate production line had run its course, that the constant trial of strength had lost its attraction and usefulness to me, that my talents and desires lay elsewhere, the lure of a regular salary proved too hard to resist. I agreed to join the office supply company.

I wanted to do well in the job, as I have always done, but I rationalised it as a financial security blanket, a means of removing the pressure I would have felt if I had been left sitting at home, wondering where I would find my customers. This way, I told myself, I had punishment–free opportunities to discover and test the new markets I wanted to enter.

So on the same day that I enrolled for duty at the office supply firm at 9am, I left at 6pm and drove in my new company car to the offices of the graphic design company. There, I agreed modest terms to provide a series of evening management training sessions in my own right – just to see if my new business could work. After four or five weeks, the company managers were so pleased with the way their business had started to develop that they recommended me to another client.

Within five months, I was making after–work visits to five or six clients and I began to realise that my new direction could actually turn out to be more lucrative than the regulation day job.

Then, if ever I needed confirmation that the future lay away from the rigid ranks of vested interests, petty jealousies and bullying which were propagated in business organisations of the day – and still survive to this – I was given it. Loud and clear.

In my day job, I reported to a divisional general manager of many years standing. He was distinguished by the fact that he always carried a large bunch of keys and made a ceremonial point of locking his office on every departure. He also kept locked the main office stationery cupboard. This seemed strange to our office staff. When they needed supplies themselves, they would go to the main warehouse rather than ask him to unlock the cupboard and be subjected to his scrutiny. Consequently, stocktaking was thrown into mayhem. I used to wonder why he had so many keys.

My key–carrying superior came into my office one day and announced that the board of directors had seconded him to run a new operation in the north. He would be away for about three months and he handed over his responsibilities to me for the duration.

My time as the stand–in went well and we achieved business growth.

I often started the day early in the office, before other staff arrived, and I began to get the impression that sometimes, somehow, I was not alone. Documents in my desk drawer appeared to have been moved, as well as sales targets, forecasts and confidential papers regarding individuals' work performance. How could this be? I always left my desk locked.

The divisional general manager returned from his secondment and I looked forward to his approval. During his absence, I had beaten every target asked of me. Within a couple of days, I was asked to prepare new targets for a board meeting. I realised the new targets were double the existing targets. It required a whole matrix of calculations and I could not see how it was going to be achievable. I enlisted the help of our field sales manager, an expert with figures and a man whom I trusted, because I 'could have tried harder' at school and maths was not my strong point.

The data was prepared and the presentation rehearsed. Because of the sensitivity of the information, we locked the material in my private filing cabinet.

On the day of the meeting in my office, I arrived 15 minutes ahead of the scheduled starting time to set up the overhead projector. The divisional general manager marshalled together the directors and the meeting began. I unlocked my filing cabinet. There was not a document in sight. The divisional regional manager accused me of running a shoddy ship, and of failing to plan and prepare during his absence. He said that I led business by 'a wing and a prayer' and pointed out to the directors that 'this is what happens when you take senior management from the dole queue'.

I didn't know how to behave. I became angry and the meeting erupted into a row. My trusty friend helped me outside to get some fresh air.

An hour later, the meeting was reconvened. The divisional regional manager informed me that the board had agreed with his view that I was incompetent, irrational and unsuitable for the job and, because I had been with the firm for less than six months, I had no rights to complain under the Industrial Relations Act. There was a show of hands and I was out. I couldn't believe it.

I returned to the company the following day to hand over my car and collect a few personal belongings. For some reason, despite myself, I decided to call in on the divisional regional manager. I don't know, perhaps it was for the desperate, remote possibility of a future reference.

Unusually, his office door was open. He must have nipped out for some reason. I went in anyway. I noticed some documents under a scattered pile of papers on his office table. They looked familiar. I took a closer look. Lying there was every one of the foils, the matrix and discussion papers that my colleague and I had prepared for the board meeting.

I didn't know what to think or what to do. One of my first reactions was to wait for his return and then march him out for a good thumping. Then I wondered if I should make a request to recall the board meeting. In the end, I simply went home, made a cup of tea and retired to the back lawn.

While I was drinking my tea and reflecting, I was visited by the mother of a family Anne and I had helped the previous Christmas. Throughout the previous weeks, she had been following my self–employment deliberations. I told her what had happened. She looked me straight in the eye and said 'stop saying if, and start saying when, you're going to begin your own business.'

Within four weeks, Anne and I had taken the leap of faith – we called it 'the divine leap' – and Michael Sylvester Associates was officially born.

It was liberating to stand on the threshold of finally doing something I wanted to do – to act on the realisation that the corporate 'straight line' was not the 'be all and end all'.

CHAPTER TWELVE

Emotional oppression and unconditional approval

All my jobs in full-time employment had been great adventures, full of challenges and hopes, but eventually they had faded into disappointment. Part of that was the way of life the salesman had to accept, but in my case, there was something else: my conditioning.

Everything had been about the 'straight line' rise up the mythical staircase to be 'the boss'. If I couldn't progress up the ladder in one company, I would go to another and try it there. When things didn't work or there was some problem, I didn't know what to do. One part of me would say: 'you've got to be the manager, you've got to be the boss' and another part of me would admit: 'actually I don't know how to do that because whenever I come up against difficult circumstances, I get into a mess'.

It was never because I couldn't do the job. I was very good in almost all of my jobs. It was emotional oppression that got me into a mess.

When I encountered emotional difficulty, I had no experience of how to handle it – only the experience I'd inherited through mother's conditioning. I would feel that I'd lost belonging or self-esteem and it would all close in on me. I would get emotionally upset or lose my temper and it would become a struggle to recover. My own behaviour would make it worse. It was like trying to beat mother: I couldn't win.

Anne recently described me as having the longest adolescence she has ever known. She has also articulated that her upbringing and experience has been the opposite to this emotional oppression. She has described her own background as one of unconditional approval.

She has viewed it as being rather dull compared to my story. It isn't. Emotional oppression lies behind my tendency to be 'intra-personal', to check my feelings before I do anything. I have found it difficult to do anything spontaneous. On many occasions, my children have urged me 'oh come on dad' – but dad had to think about it. It has to feel right for me before I make any approach.

Understandably, Anne gets fed up with with the preoccupation I have about my 'intra-personal' feelings, with my being self-centred.

Anne is inter-personal, gregarious – a product, she has said, of the unconditional approval she received from her parents Ken and Nancy. They had a 'you can do it' attitude. They might have had differences of opinion over how to do it, but that had nothing to do with the underlying message 'we love you, get on with it'. Well, my parents loved me, but they wanted to control me all the time. So I understand that my behaviour has been frustrating to someone like Anne, it's almost been like holding one back.

While mother and I were no longer having regular direct contact throughout the crises in my various positions of full-time employment, her conditioning remained inside my head. I never got free of her. She remained on the periphery but she still commanded a lot of power.

Wherever I was, I would behave like her in a way. I brought my mother's behaviour into our marriage. I'd make terms and conditions and expect Anne to comply. It was stupid. I must have given Anne a hell of a time. As if she wasn't receiving a bad enough time on the irregular occasions my mother did make an appearance. . .

When Anne and I first got married, we would alternate Sunday visits between mother and dad and Anne's parents. The visits to Anne's parents were great. We usually ended up in a pub somewhere and thoroughly enjoyed each other's company, it was a pleasure. The visits to mother and dad felt like a duty. Mother's behaviour was dreadful. There was a growing consciousness I didn't want to go and I felt sorry for my dad in that. We carried on the formalities but it began to play less and less a part in my life. But I never had the strength to say 'I don't want to see you again'. I wasn't like that and society wasn't like that.

In the summer months, each set of parents would also visit us. Dad helped me with our garden. It was a massive piece of land, almost like a field. I didn't know what I was doing. Dad showed me. Anne's dad was brilliant at fixing things, so both dad and Ken were always supportive in that sort of way.

But mother always gave off the impression that nothing was ever good enough. She made Anne's life a misery. It went on while we had our children and continued until James and Julian became teenagers.

The contrast was best illustrated by an episode following another of my unfulfilled periods of employment, this time with a precision watch manufacturer in London. This company promoted ruthless selling methods. I shouldn't have joined them. I gave it a go but I didn't do very well, and my brief sojourn ended in traumatic fashion. I rang up one day and they simply told me I was being sacked because I hadn't done enough. It was a Friday. I was told to return my company car to London by the following Monday and after that, I was finished.

It knocked me for six. Anne and I wondered what we were going to do. So we called a family meeting at mother and dad's on the Sunday and sat round the coal fire, trying to work something out. Nancy and Ken were in the discussion, as was dad and even Auntie Gwen. But mother was not. She hovered about on the fringe of the get-together.

Ken said 'I'm not going to work tomorrow, Anne will go with you to London, I'll go as well, we'll follow you down, you can sort it out, hand your car over and Anne and I will bring you back'. What a marvellous thing to put themselves out like that. Dad said 'I'll go to the solicitors on Monday morning and seek advice. I don't know what they'll say but I'll find someone to explain the situation'. I ended up coping with an awkward situation extremely well because I knew I'd got all this love and support.

From everyone except mother. From her, I had inherited a conditioning that, when I considered somebody was coming on to me in what I deemed to be a bullying way, it pushed me into child ego and a desire to retaliate without thinking about it.

So when it came to starting my own business, the feeling of liberation from this conditioning was tempered by an acknowledgement that my new direction would require a conscious effort to adjust my behaviour.

It was a requirement of which I had become increasingly aware. I remember it being highlighted by an episode towards the end of my second spell with the electrical spares manufacturer.

I was in my mid–30s and one of the salespeople I managed, let's call him Bob, was in his late 50s. He had been with the business a long time and was a highly–respected salesperson, but you could see that his performance was slipping.

I had come to pride myself on organisation and systems and, when it came to his expenses, Bob would throw my system, my precious system, out of order. Instead of receiving all the documentation at the same time, I would receive all the receipts the first week, all the expense forms the following week, and some more missed–off receipts the week after. But that was not the worst about him, from my point of view.

With my background in clothing, and my insistence on smart appearance, I was horrified every time I met Bob in the field and noticed that his tie was constantly askew and often over his shoulder. Months went by and our relationship got worse. I thought 'I'm going to sort him out, he's going'. But a colleague took me to one side and said 'Michael, I think there's another way of going about this'.

I knew Bob and his wife and I liked them both, but because I was 'his boss', I thought I had to behave differently and force him to tow the line.

I went to see Bob at his home and, instead of asserting myself, I sat down to ask him open questions and to listen. I knew he had two adolescent sons, both with learning difficulties, who were always away at a special boarding school. What I had not appreciated was that Bob's father had always paid for the school fees, but he had died. The money was no longer there so Bob was in a dilemma. Did he pull out his boys from of a boarding school that he could not afford, with all the implications that would have for their education, or did he work himself to death to find enough money to keep them there?

In his quandary, he had opted for working himself to death.

He had got himself into a terrible state of worry and anxiety. He was unable to sleep at night and it was having an effect on his work performance. After a sleepless night, he would be in a muddle the next morning, and would not check himself in a mirror before he left the house. He did not know that he appeared unshaven or that his tie was askew. He was frightened.

When I found all this out, my view towards him became quite different. If Bob had been a key accounts salesperson, required to 'meet and greet' and to make presentations, his appearance would have been important. But he wasn't. He had regular appointments with retail shops all around Essex and Hertfordshire to check all the stock. He would work out a suggested order, introduce new lines and promotions to the shopkeeper, and merchandise the stock when it came in. If he came across any faulty parts, he would remove them and issue customers with a credit.

He was totally honest, totally trustworthy, and the customers thought he was wonderful. He could have been wearing overalls, for all they were concerned.

When I understood this, I realised that it wasn't Bob who had to change, it was me.

I'd got to let go of towing the line, wriggle free of the straitjacket of accepted methods and use some creativity. I helped him, I encouraged others to work with him and we shared responsibility. It strengthened the team.

Bob worked his way back up to being one of the company's top salesmen again. And I learned valuable lessons that would lay down fairer and more rewarding foundations for Michael Sylvester Associates.

CHAPTER THIRTEEN

From the Bottom up

I'm sure the following observation will strike a chord with everyone who has set up his or her own business. It's about where your work comes from. . . it's rarely where you think it's going to come from.

In my first weeks as Michael Sylvester Associates, I recognised that, although I enjoyed a small customer base, it could not generate a substantial income. In addition to having no major customers, I had no capital support, no premises, marginal parental interest, no car and no business partners with whom to discuss ideas and developments. So I gathered around me a group of individuals who respected me and upon whom I could call for guidance. They were all ex–officio, so they could be called on for unbiased opinion and direction.

This group included Les Sylvester, my dad, who had agreed to be my mentor, even though he was uncomfortable with my venture.

I converted part of my home into a study to give me instant access to my business and maximise working time. I begged and borrowed wherever and whatever I could and managed with the minimum.

During this start–up period, another major decision was taken concerning Anne. She decided to return to work in the civil service, which she had left nine years earlier to look after our children, James and Julian. James was soon to enter comprehensive school – neither of our sons was to follow my ill–conceived path into private education – and Julian was thriving at pre–school nursery. Anne's return to work would provide a secure income for the family in potentially uncertain times.

I thought that finding customers for Michael Sylvester Associates was going to come from making a multitude of contacts wherever I could through the national and international networks. When it comes to the search for customers, we follow these conventional guidelines and routes.

But my breakthrough came from Bottom House Farm at the other end of my own village.

A friend of the family, Mary, called in. She was employed to do a spot of housekeeping for a mutual acquaintance, who was the managing director of a healthcare company based at the farm. Mary passed on an invitation to drop in at their offices for another chat.

So I strolled down the road and struck up a conversation with their finance director. He also happened to be self–employed: the healthcare company was just one of a number of businesses he represented. I thought it was just an informal chat and they were interested in my welfare. But towards the end of the conversation, the finance director said 'well I know there's no point in trying to offer you a job because you've convinced me that you want to start up your own business'. This came as something of an encouragement. I was still unsure I had convinced myself. He proceeded to ask how much I needed to run my business. I referred to my business plan: £260 a week. He said 'right, I'll give you £260 for three days' work a week, I'll give you a car – you can pay your own private mileage – and we'll pay immediately on receipt of your invoice'. I thought there must be a catch. I asked him what the company wanted me to do.

He outlined responsibilities to accompany the managing director on customer visits and teach her how to sell. Her unrivalled background in medicine, especially in health screening which was attractive to corporate business and big insurance companies, gave her open invitations to seminars, conferences, board meetings and presentations with the captains of industry. But she had difficulties in closing a deal. I was charged with showing her how it was done. We toured the country visiting prospective clients and she became the company's top sales person.

Who'd have thought that my starting point would have been Bottom House Farm? I had called in with no agenda. I've often thought since that if I had treated it as a job interview, I would have got it entirely wrong. I would have put on my best suit and been all starchy and got nowhere. The occasion called for acting and working flexibly. I had never thought like that before; I hadn't considered it allowable or possible.

The finance director gave me other marketing assignments. At the same time, I picked up where I had left off with the graphic design company. I worked for them on Mondays, for the healthcare company on Tuesdays, Wednesdays and Thursdays, I lectured on marketing for two evenings a week at the local college and at weekends, I followed up adverts I had placed in the evening paper.

Before long, Fridays were also taken up with a contract to help a local start–up business that manufactured motifs for fashion clothing. Sadly, it had lost its owner to unexpected death. I helped the owner's 21–year–old son take over management of two small factories with around 30 employees. I set up weekly board meetings, eventually letting the son take the chair. I also brought in a young salesman whose career I had been observing for some time. I introduced him to Marks & Spencer in London's West End. We contacted other big retail names. Within six months, we had cornered the market for quality designs. We then progressed to cosmetics and screen printing.

Turnover, profit and employees were all increased.

My first year was a complete success but I reached the point of being unable to take on more business without beginning to employ staff, which finances would not permit. I agreed a wind down procedure with the healthcare company and joined the Chamber of Commerce to run training courses for their members covering a wide range of management topics.

One of the delegates was the senior partner of a management college shortly to open in the Midlands. He and his partners were looking for someone to brand their business externally and internally. After a year, the business had accumulated a team of outside consultants and the college was full of delegates attending residential courses in management services. I was asked to set up a programme of development for company directors. I opened a small office in the college. reduced my capacity with the graphic designers and motif manufacturers and helped a group of business people offer support to long–term unemployed with the aim of getting them back into work. This involved working with clients on a one–to–one basis, confidence building, coaching and mentoring. I found the work completely stimulating.

I was approached by a major building company to help design a full training programme for its growing ranks of employees. I was now working with a small team of specialist trainers. We covered seminars, round robin presentations, negotiation and role–play from training in childcare residential homes to project management in the defence industry. We were completely independent and given the freedom to speak openly and honestly, a vast contrast to the strictures of office politics I had experienced in full–time employment. We were committed to helping people to do better for themselves. We encouraged individuals in the areas of self–confidence, problem–solving and improved communication.

Helped by two members of the specialist trainers, I won a contract to carry out training and development work for the market leader in agricultural machine manufacturing. For the following five years, we ran all external training for the company and helped it to launch the new generation of combine harvesters.

In my third year as Michael Sylvester Associates, a former colleague contacted me with an invitation to join an international training organisation. It had attracted major clients, all with a mass audience for training in new skills. He needed to assemble a team to service the contracts. These included an exceptionally large commitment to train every single member of staff at venues across the country for a high profile insurance company. I worked with the organisation as course director and we fulfilled our first brief successfully. I was then asked to undertake a series of additional follow–up schemes for the company, including the undergraduate programme, management development and investigating the retail market.

We had really hit the big time as far as I was concerned. Within two or three years, I was presenting at the International Press Centre in London to a gathering of 1,000 – an hour-and-a-half stand-up without any visual aids. I spoke to the audience about some of the conflicts I've found in people's businesses and it related to everybody in the room. I got a rousing round of applause. People approached me at the end to express their appreciation. That was a huge moment, because while I was travelling on the train to the engagement, my mother was inside my head saying 'you can't do this, what are you doing?' But I did it, and I did it well.

After the applause, the delegates departed to a smoked salmon lunch. I was left completely alone on the stage, highly elated, over-excited. I leapt from the stage shouting 'yes', without realising I was still fastened to my roving microphone lead. It hauled me back, and in the moment of shock, I let forth an involuntary expletive. Of course, not only was I fastened to the microphone, but the microphone was still on, so my discomfort was volubly broadcast to the delegates as an accompaniment to their lunch.

I was also invited to present at the Barbican. This was an even bigger event for company accountants and finance directors. Instead of entering from the wings, I sat in the audience watching the lead-up to my introduction, then I walked down through the audience and climbed on to the stage. Everybody wondered what was going on. I took them through six points of establishing two-way communication. The sixth point was about punctuation. Afterwards, I received a letter of complaint. One director said he and his team left early, insulted at the inclusion of a talk about punctuation for such a large fee. The letter contained 23 spelling mistakes and the secretary had misspelt the director's name. . .

The leader of the international training organisation asked us to become more involved with the group but we declined. Such a large provider leans towards prescriptive approaches. I preferred to continue running my own smaller business to enable my team and I to use our creativity and common sense approach on more specialist contracts.

In January 2000, I was nearing the end of my time working with the international training organisation. Trade was falling away, something I had anticipated a year or two earlier, and I had drawn up plans for new directions. But our group leader wouldn't accept anything about alternative thinking, adapting to new trends or going about business in a different way.

It was all set to spark a profound sequence of events.

CHAPTER FOURTEEN

Bullying: the last stand

I have a theory forged by the memory of being chased home by my primary school tormentors, shaped further by my suffering in the atmosphere of being 'bottom of the barrel' at secondary school and polished off by several subsequent workplace experiences.

It is that when you've been bullied, you feel as though you've been marked down as a victim. And you can give it off as a signal.

It was certainly picked up by the two lads who encountered me as a gauche newcomer, still in school uniform, on the third or fourth day of my first job at Dixon & Parker. The lads were from a notorious district of Nottingham called The Meadows. Our paths crossed in the yard. I was a bit frightened of them and they sensed it. I realised that they were planning to give me a welcome to remember.

I couldn't cope with the thought and I turned to my dad. He told me that he understood, but at the same time, I had to accept that it was going to happen and there was no way out. I wouldn't be able to run away, so it was absolutely essential to land the first punch myself.

I'm not that way inclined at all. So he taught me how to do it. He said to act quickly, because as soon as my aggressor realised I was going to make a move, he would take evasive action and I would miss. He told me to grab hold of the aggressor's shirt or warehouse coat with my left hand, gripping it so tightly that he could not move, then to punch him with my right hand on the bridge of his nose. The blow had to be so powerful that his nose might break, and there would be blood everywhere, or his eyes would water, so he couldn't see what was happening. Then I had to hit and hit and hit again and make a lot of noise and get out however I could.

I was terrified and dad knew it. So he made me an offer: 'It's my half day off work tomorrow. I'll come and wait outside the front door of Dixon's. When you come out at half past five and you've had a problem, I'll sort it out and finish it off, but you must signal to me that you've had a go. If you haven't succeeded then OK, I'll do the job, but you must signal because I'm not touching anybody unless you've had a go.'

On the day, I was getting into a lift when the lads appeared and followed me in. It was a goods lift with a chain door that had to be pulled across. Between the second and third floors, they threw back the door, bringing the lift to a halt. There was no way out. I was trapped in the brick surrounds of the shaft and they set about me. I put my dad's plan into action and created such a noise that, by the time the lift was started again and reached the top floor, a crowd of employees had gathered to help me tackle the lads and the melee had to be broken up by a manager.

At half past five, I emerged from the factory door and there was my dad, standing across the road wearing his windcheater, an open–necked shirt and with his hands in his pockets. A mild, simplistic man, extremely strong, but a man who didn't drink, or smoke or like a lot of fuss. He was looking. I can see the look now. I thought, 'what a hero'. He had no idea what was coming out that door, how many, how big or strong, how ruthless, it didn't matter. He would have done something about it there in the street. I signalled 'dad I've done it', we got in the car and went home. He never said 'well done'. But I loved him for being there.

You might think that was the moment I overcame my susceptibility to bullying, that from the age of 16 I could hold my head high and advance fearlessly in the big, wide world.

But as you know by now, a constant battle has raged beneath the surface of my working and personal life. Emotional oppression has ensured that, in the back of my mind, in the pit of my stomach, there's always Michael the complete failure, the complete reject – I mean, what else could you expect. It's behaviour that I have caught. It's my mother telling me I can't do it. At the same time, this conditioning has triggered a counter behaviour, one of 'who are you telling I can't do that, well, I'll have a go'.

So there was a day I finally overcame the bullying. It wasn't when I was 16. It was when I was in my mid 50s. And it centred around the end of my time with the international training organisation.

The leader of the organisation was facing up to changing markets by going 'intra–business', thinking he was doing his best to save costs by undergoing reviews and carrying out all sorts of checks and balances. This included a series of interviews with each member of the group which, in many cases, resulted in them having their work taken away. We all had a picture in our mind of a wild west gunslinger, slowly circling a town with a ready aim to shoot down anyone who appeared at the window, or let their cover slip in any way.

My turn came to go for this dreaded interview. I was extremely wound up about it. As much as a week ahead of the appointment, I warned my son James I might end up hitting the leader. Naturally, he told me this wouldn't be a good idea, but I was trying to express my obsession with the scenario.

I had a valued friend at the time who devoted his time to talking me through aspects of assertiveness and behaviour in terms of saying sorry. It was extraordinarily helpful, a technique for appearing to apologise – 'I'm sorry you should feel that way', 'I'm sorry the market's affecting you like this' – when, in fact, it wasn't an apology at all.

On the day, my meeting with the leader lasted about three hours. He was really quite insulting towards me. There was a period after two hours when the lift shaft experience of all those years before flashed across my mind.

I found myself in a position where I could have once again followed dad's instructions, grabbed hold of the leader's shirt and proceeded to unleash the telling blows. I could feel it happening.

However, I managed to control myself and return to my adviser's assertiveness strategies. Eventually, the leader appeared to lose interest and concentration and I emerged from the meeting unscathed.

To be more precise, it felt as if I had emerged from the meeting triumphant. As I was driving home, my head was full of what had happened and I wanted to tell someone: 'I've actually handled this. For the first time, I've actually sorted it out.'

I had an idea to drive across Nottingham to tell my dad, but he was a very old man at this time, he was 92. So I opted for the next best thing.

I called in at Jimmy Onions' butcher shop on the way home in Ratcliffe – a throwback to dad's butcher days. These were 'the lads' as far as I was concerned and it felt good to be in their company. Amongst other things, I told them about my success, not all the detail, and then I drove home.

That same evening, probably close to being that same hour, my dad poured a glass of whisky, took it with him upstairs to his front bedroom, settled down for a rest – and died.

It's tempting and probably a bit corny to draw this sentimental conclusion. The following day, the doctor told me he'd have no difficulty in attributing dad's death to 'old age'.

To my mind, though, it's almost as if dad had decided: 'At last, Michael's got control of himself. I can go now'.

CHAPTER FIFTEEN

The butcher and the butcher's boy

On the day of dad's funeral, I wore the same suit I had picked out for the confrontation with the group leader – replacing a red tie (to denote anger with a bully) with a black tie, of course, to denote the befitting respect.

I was standing on the steps of the old family house at Toton with my son James, drawing on a cigarette while waiting for the hearse to arrive, when it occurred to me. I turned to James and shared the thought: 'do you know, in all my life, I don't think he ever said well done'. James did not have time to respond. At that moment, the hearse pulled into view and we all took up our positions for the procession to the crematorium.

My dear dad. One of the last in the line of the Victorians.

Grandad Arthur was born in Queen Victoria's reign and ran his household in an authoritarian way, albeit he was a socialist, so dad was brought up with that type of thinking and behaviour. He wasn't as strict as Arthur, but he retained a good deal of the formalities of the time.

Dad wasn't an open man and could not be described as at all dynamic. With him, it was solidity, feet on the ground, common sense. I must have upset him and disappointed him, but he never went on about it. I would know I had done something wrong by his demeanour. He was not an ambitious person, other than when a young man, wanting to win a sports game. He was not a financial person, He didn't understand money or how to use it. Dad just knew you had money in the bank and you only spent what you had got. He never borrowed. He did not have any savings until very late in life, when he inherited a small amount.

I remembered when I had left private school, with little to show for the education in which he had invested so heavily. He said to me 'well, that's been a right bloody waste of time, you'll never have another penny out of me'. And I never did.

But he also made it clear: 'if you want to talk to somebody, I'll help you along – I'll put you in touch with people'. And we did that, Anne and I, several times. He never got involved with our business but we could always go and talk to him about things. He was exceptionally good like that.

There was one particularly good example, when I had made the 'big time' – in both my eyes and his – as temporary replacement manager at the hosiery manufacturers in Leicester.

I had been warned of the existence of a big security problem. A lot of theft was taking place. I was told: 'when you go in there, mate, you've got to hit it fast and you've got to hit it hard'. The company imported a lot of cotton underwear from Portugal. The product was delivered in massive trucks and, after some months, I began to realise that this was the source of the stock shortage. It wasn't being stolen from the warehouse itself, but it had something to do with the truck delivery. I wondered what I could do about it, who I could talk to about it. I went to the best place I knew. My dad.

He advised me in great detail. He said: 'look out for the truck arriving earlier than the appointed time and for the driver wanting it to be tipped there and then because he wants to go back to Portugal. Your people will want to help him, it will be very urgent to unload the stock, so it might not be checked that carefully. When the truck arrives early for tipping, turn him away, say you haven't got the men available and tell him to return at the appointed time. Then get everything set up, all your conveyors and all your people, and you've got to be on the unloading dock yourself, take a clipboard, stand there and tick off every box as you see it coming down the chute. Expect an interruption. Somebody will come up to you to take your focus off watching, and onto another urgent matter. So tell your secretary it doesn't matter who rings, whether it's the boss or whoever, don't take any calls. You must not be disturbed while you're watching this process.'

At the appointed time, I stood on the dock with my clipboard. There were about 15 men around the driver. I ticked off the boxes as they came down the chute, then I looked more carefully and noticed that the boxes were being moved inside the truck. My people were helping to turn the boxes to face a different way from time to time. At this point, my secretary approached me and said 'there's a phone call'. I told her: 'I can't take it'. Why were my own people suddenly looking at me a bit oddly? When the next box came down, I shouted for the conveyer belt to be stopped, and walked across to take a closer look. I turned it back the other way and the belt resumed. I kept a close watch and spotted another suspicious box. Again, I shouted 'stop'. I walked across, turned the box around, and returned to the dock, where it became apparent I was being crowded out, and could have been pushed off. They were all in it together. All the tampered boxes had got a fist–hole in the side. The previous night, at a service station perhaps, people had boarded the truck, punched through the boxes and grabbed £20 worth of stock here and there. From that point on, the thieving stopped.

Dad would have been able to predict the scenario because, as well as the solid side to him, the sense of humour, there was also a roguish side. He was willing and able to pull the odd trick, particularly if it righted a wrong in his mind.

One Christmas, a social club approached dad as the butcher at the Co-op and explained that it was about to host a season of dinners for all the local factories. Dad was asked if he could come up with a deal for supplying all the turkeys. He passed on the order to the butchery manager and asked him to produce a good price. The manager refused to bend the rules. 'They can pay the same price as everyone else'.

Dad felt a bit embarrassed because he'd been asked as a friend. So he got together with his mates. At the Co-op slaughter house, vans would arrive at different times to be loaded with meat. Dad and his mates organised a convoy of five vans to arrive at the same time and to create a chaotic scene in which these all had to be loaded at the same time. One of the vans was not to set off on a Co-op meat round – its destination was the social club, with a consignment of all the turkeys it wanted for Christmas, without a penny going to the Co-op.

On another occasion – a terrible story nowadays, but funny to look back on – I would arrive home to a house full of turkeys in different stages of meltdown. Customers would pay more for a fresh turkey than frozen, so dad would bring the frozen birds home, leave them all out to adjust to room temperature, then sell them as fresh, pocketing the difference.

And dad was responsible for my earliest introduction to profit. When I was 11, during the school holidays, I would accompany him on his meat deliveries around the Nottinghamshire villages. I would be 'butcher's boy' for the day. I was given a striped apron and a wicker basket. My job would be to walk up all the long paths to the houses, take the orders and return to the van where dad and Ken Ralston, 'his lad', would prepare the meat, wrap it in greaseproof paper and put it in the basket, along with the bill. I would return up the path, deliver the order and take the payment – along with the inevitable sixpence for the butcher's boy. I thought it was a really good scheme. I also thought I was being helpful because there were certain people who couldn't get out of their house, and up and down their drive. And I would adopt a caring manner accordingly. I didn't realise that dad and Ken were giving me the longest paths to walk up and down because it enabled them to do the others much quicker.

Dad had a wonderful reputation with his customers. He used to ask them: 'what do you want today, what do you want for Sunday?' They might say: 'well I've got visitors coming around, somebody special, what have you got?' My dad would say 'I've got a very nice beef here, or some pork'. They wouldn't be able to make up their minds and they'd ask him what was best.

'Do you want my professional opinion, or my personal opinion?'

'Oh, your personal opinion'.

'I wouldn't have that. . .'

His recommendation would put another sixpence on his bill. And as the customers went out the door, he'd say 'now if it doesn't eat good, make sure you bring it back'.

He used to call it his pyschology. He'd have a bit of fun with his staff and his customers. He made them feel good.

My friends use to call him Les the boots, because when he was at home he was always walking around in wellington boots in the garden, planting his flowers. All of my pals thought the world of him, because he thought the world of them. When I was 16, I wanted to introduce him to my best pal, Chris Mines. I was apprehensive because Chris was a biker, a rocker, a bit on the wild side. I thought my dad would disapprove. Chris had just bought a car and I told him to call round. It was a springtime Sunday morning, the time for bedding plants to be put in. Dad was pottering around as usual and had placed a row of seed boxes in a straight line all the way down the drive. As he was making his way back to the house for a cup of tea, I saw Chris's car turn into the drive, and carry forwards, and forwards, and forwards over every single seed box. There were about a dozen boxes in all, and they were all broken into splinters. Chris brought his car to a halt at the very top of the drive and removed his tall frame from the driver's seat, bearing a huge grin. I wished for a large hole to appear and to swallow me up. My dad re–emerged from the house and surveyed the ruins, walked up to Chris, shook him by the hand – and they got on famously from that minute.

They were all at his funeral. Chris, Ken Ralston and the butchery manager from the Co–op. And, as always by my side, Anne. Wife, mother of two great sons, Devoted, supportive. By this time we had shared almost 30 years of marriage. I can still remember how it felt to fall in love with her.

After the service, we all returned to dad's home for a get–together – the kind of party, it crossed my mind, he could have had when he was still alive. But there was always mother's reactions.

These reactions dated back to the beginning of their married life. Mother and dad married in the cathedral in Derby Road, Nottingham, just before the outbreak of the Second World War. The plan was for them to drive to the fishing village of Crinan, in Argyll, for their honeymoon and stay with dad's friends, the MacDonalds. Dad had got a little car, an Austin Ruby, the only one on his street. On the road north, it broke down on the A1 at Blyth. They managed to get it to a garage in Doncaster, where they were told it would be some days before it would be in working order again, so they actually ended up staying in a little village pub near Filey, in Yorkshire. They never made it to their original honeymoon destination. They never attempted to again. Mother pointedly refused to celebrate her wedding anniversary from then on. She would ridicule dad about it. Even when Anne and I had worked out it must have been their 60th wedding anniversary, she absolutely refused to entertain it.

Mother's reactions continued right through to the end of their married life. When it was my dad's 90th birthday, I cooked a meal for him at my home in Langar. In honour of the master butcher, we had a whole loin of pork with all the trimmings. We filled the kitchen with his relatives and friends. But mother said she wouldn't attend, so dad said he didn't think he could either. Anne took matters into her own hands and suggested: 'well Les, why don't you come along without her? I'll fetch you in the car.' For the first time of which I'm aware in his life, he agreed to do something without mother. He turned up, had a few whiskies, a couple of glasses of wine with the food, and we had a fabulous evening.

What a burden for the old man. Dad and his family did everything they could to include mother in what was a very big Victorian family, but she excluded herself mentally. She kept herself on the outside, looking in. She would go through the motions – cooking and caring for people if they weren't well – but behind their backs, she would deride every single person.

Auntie Gwen does not think dad knew about mother's affairs and says he must have been hurt a great deal by her. Apparently he was frightened to confront her in case mother left him. Gwen believes that dad would have been unprepared to have been able to look after me alone, so his suffering could have no closure.

There are occasions when I feel that dad is within me, and I am him – when I'm working with a person, or small group, usually when somebody's uncomfortable for some reason, perhaps suffering with a work problem. I feel that I've got that persona of having a bit of fun, or being able to make them feel comfortable, or talking them through a potential hazard.

At dad's funeral, I began to feel a responsibility to do what I felt he would have wanted me to do – to look after mother, to take control and organise her affairs and make sure she was well cared for.

My dear dad. One of the last in the line of the Victorians. And I'm one of the last trying to sort it all out.

The new generation seems less tainted by this emotional oppression. They have broken the mould. They are free.

As friends and relatives were leaving the funeral reception, my son James, who had been standing with me on the steps of the house in Toton before the hearse arrived, once again appeared at my side and said: 'well done, dad'.

CHAPTER SIXTEEN

Goodnight Irene

I don't know when Renee decided that she wanted to become known as Irene. The first time this new identity came to my attention was in a phone call from the police.

It was about a year after I had resolved to forgive her and to try to restore some sort of relationship with her. My dad had gone, and I wanted to love her, to cuddle her, to be closer to her. She had never got on with her grandchildren and I wanted to involve her and to make all that better. I wanted to be her son and I wanted her to be my mother.

I would visit her at least once a week, taking a little something for her each time and a book for myself to read while she had a bath. She liked me to be close at hand. She was frightened she might slip or fall or not be able to get out of the bath.

She would cook a meal. As well as thinking it was a good way for her to eat properly – because on your own, you don't want to do that much – I felt it gave her a purpose. And I enjoyed the meal anyway. Sometimes, she would buy cod or plaice from the fish van that used to tour the area from Grimsby. She would cook mashed potato and peas and some parsley sauce. It would be a big piece of fish, very homely, and she would provide a childlike pudding, like bananas and custard.

There would be three chairs at the table, one for mother, one for me, and dad's chair remained. We would sit and talk. It was rather nice. We would chuckle about things. I always tried to get her to laugh about something. I would chat about what I was doing at work and what her grandchildren were doing.

It was the closest I had ever been to her since, I suppose, I was her little boy. I was trying to get back the years. It was like being a teenager with her and growing up again. But I never got there. The anger resurfaced.

The first signs of change came after I had been working at the Cabinet Office in London – a contract of which I had been particularly proud. Instead of going home to Langar one night, I went instead to visit her at Toton and share my pride and excitement.

She responded to my story with a phrase that brought back the days of 'could have tried harder' and of thinking I had upset her. She said: 'What could you possibly teach them?' It cut through me. From that moment on, our relationship started to go downhill.

My weekly visits began to take peculiar turns of events. She would say things I didn't understand. On one occasion, she turned to me and vowed: 'I'll get my own back on you'.

She insisted on Auntie Gwen going to the bank because she said I had stolen all her money. I tackled mother about it but it triggered screaming and tears. Anne became the target of accusations and solicitors became involved.

Where had her money gone? Well, it hadn't gone anywhere. Every week on my visits, I had taken her bank accounts with me and gone through all the numbers with her. There were about five bank accounts. I don't know why the money was in all different accounts, but there it was. Each week, she couldn't understand it. It got worse and worse and worse.

One Saturday morning, I received a letter from her solicitors. It informed me that my power of attorney had been revoked and I no longer had any right of access to her financial details. I couldn't look after her, I couldn't make sure her bills were paid.

She wouldn't tell me who had taken over the responsibility. She led me to believe it was her niece's husband, who was an ex–bank manager, She never actually mentioned his name. We knew somebody was talking to her but we didn't know who it was.

I struggled to contain a sense of rage and vengeance. My mother had rejected me. Rejected me in my 50s. Despite our so–called maturity, it is just as painful being rejected in our later years.

Anne and I continued to visit her but it always ended in a row. We were accused of this, that and the other. It was absolutely bloody awful.

I had a feeling that there was something wrong with her finances, but I didn't know exactly what it was. I had a feeling that amounts were being taken out of her account. We tried and tried and tried to talk to her but she wouldn't speak to us, the solicitor wouldn't speak to us, no–one would talk to us about it. In the end, it became almost impossible to meet her.

I became convinced she had a spell on me.

Then came the phone call from the police. They had received 999 calls on two occasions from 'Irene' and the police were concerned. I spoke to the officer who taken one of the calls and he told me it was something to do with money being extorted. He referred to a 'handyman'.

I went to my mother's house and tried to have a conversation with her. I knew of a 'handyman' who had been a friend of my dad and had supplied the service for many years – and been well paid for it. He would do other things as well, like take mother shopping. In fact, we had developed a feeling that he hadn't liked me for some time. He had been quite awkward with me on some of my visits.

Within half–an–hour of calling upon mother, I'd realised. She'd made him power of attorney. He had cleared out all her bank accounts and transferred the total – £16,000 – into an account in his own name, so she couldn't touch it. He had a pension book, so on pension day, he'd draw an amount and return to mother's house with a little bag of groceries and some change – which she thought was her pension.

I called a locksmith to the house to change the locks. I also contacted the local police myself.

I felt outrage towards mother. I just wanted to get her out of the house, into hospital, wherever. But I found myself making her a cup of tea.

It was a dark late afternoon in October and she said: 'He will be here in a minute'. I said: 'All right mum, why's that then?'

'He always comes just after it's dark and then he goes upstairs in the drawers and deals with things up there'.

The locksmith was still at work, I sensed mother was agitated and I was downright angry. Then I heard the locksmith say: 'Hello, who are you?'

And the 'handyman' made his entrance. He said: 'What's going on here?' I placed my arm firmly around his shoulder and frogmarched him down the drive and under the street lights. My mind darted between the alternatives of simply talking to him or punching his head off. I don't know why the second didn't happen. So I began talking to him.

His first words were: 'I told your mum when she had this idea, I told her it wouldn't work.' The conversation did not go on much further before a constable arrived in response to my call.

The 'handyman' was subsequently investigated and well and truly warned off. We did not take any legal action.

In the following months, mother became ill and had a small stroke. It became clear that she couldn't take care of herself.

It was New Year's Day, mother was in hospital, and Anne and I went to her house to get some clothing for her.

Anne went upstairs to the underwear drawer. She re-emerged and said: 'I think you'd better have a look at this'. In the drawer, she had come across a new will made by mother. It left everything to the 'handyman'.

That's why he had always 'gone upstairs to deal with things'. He had been trying to find a copy of the will. For some reason, whether he hadn't thought it would be there, or he didn't like to go there, he hadn't looked in the underwear drawer. He thought he would have got all the money and the house. He couldn't have known that I owned the house.

It was the final insult. Mother went into interim care while we used her solicitors to get power of attorney back and to sort out the will. After a lot of effort, the solicitor agreed to send a member of his team to meet mother and I to sign the necessary papers.

I had a sixth sense. I said: 'Just before you sign that, mum, can I have a look at it?' The solicitor had made power of attorney out to himself. The solicitor's representative said: 'Sorry, I'm just doing what I've been asked to do'. Over the next few days, it transpired that the solicitor had known the 'handyman'.

Over the years, mother might have said that she trusted me, but clearly she didn't. She must have trusted my dad, because he never did anything to break that. I think he was frightened she would have a tantrum.

Recently, before going on holiday, I went to see mother at the care home because I wanted a clear conscience while I was away. She was fine when I arrived but, within minutes, went into a sort of hysterical spasm, crying, silently screaming, acting as though in pain. I became alarmed at seeing this misery and felt helpless at being unable to console her. I called a nurse, then two more arrived. They tried hard to get her to relax but she had a firm grip on the chair. One of the nurses said: "This only happens when you come, Michael. She is all right the rest of the time."

I went to the toilet and I was sick.

On subsequent visits, I began to get quite cross with her. I would find her with her hair done and her teeth in, sitting up in a wheelchair trying to feed herself. It meant that, time after time, she was missing slots in the diary for her funeral.

For almost a year, we were told to expect her to die. Continually, both the doctor and the care home would give us deadlines of as little as 48 hours.

Because I felt I wouldn't be able to predict where my emotions might take me at the appointed hour, I went out and found an undertaker to sort out all the arrangements in advance. I kept all the details in a bag and I carried them with me everywhere. I wouldn't even have had to go and get the death certificate. I did this so that, when it finally happened, I could deal exclusively with all the grief mother's death might bring.

It has been put to me that this was a cool and insensitive preparation. But I had reached despair over the agonies she had caused me and my family. Years and years of it. I accept that, ultimately, there might have been a part played by dementia, but I maintain that she had a strong sense of bitterness and antagonism which permeated this.

Renee died on 11 March, 2009. I arranged the funeral for April Fool's Day.

For six months following the service, I stopped going to church. I decided I wanted a complete break from it. Since the day we buried Renee, I have not had one 'visit' from her, like I had sensed my dad 'returning' two or three times – a breeze-like sensation, as if he were brushing past me, as if he were still real.

Instead, I was in almost continual physical pain – with what was diagnosed as a form of gout and with extreme discomfort caused by pressure bearing down on my rib cage. I was reminded of mother's vow – 'I'll get my own back on you' – and I have wondered if that was what she was trying to do from afar, the actions of a lost soul.

There are other occasions when, I'm not going to say I shed a tear, but I think it's a great shame and very sad. But to this day, I don't have any deep sentimentality about Renee in the way I have continued to do so about my dad.

CHAPTER SEVENTEEN

Going around in circles

My work as a trainer and mentor has never been about giving people a finite result – 'come here and learn this'. That's not an encouragement to do anything. My work has always been about motivation, about saying 'if you're now interested, go out into life and find the next page for yourself'. I don't even define the size of the page. You can lead a horse to water but you cannot make it drink. My job is to make the horse thirsty.

I have been fascinated by the thoughts of key people who have observed the way we behave and work – in particular, great American thinkers such as Douglas McGregor and Frederick Hertzberg. And, of course, Abraham Maslow.

Maslow was a social scientist, who came up with a groundbreaking theory of what causes motivation and how it works. It became paramount to marketing-related issues in the 70s. Yet Maslow looked at this in the late 50s and 60s. It took all those years and years for people to accept it.

He formulated his thinking, so it was easier for people to understand. He came up with a phrase, a 'hierarchy of needs', and he used a triangular diagram, a pyramid, to demonstrate it.

Maslow's hierarchy has been extremely widely documented and I do not believe I'm in a position to challenge or embroider what he came up with. The following is simply my interpretation of the hierarchy, a reference to how it remains as relevant today as when Maslow first produced it.

But I also believe that we are beginning to see different shapes take place.

Maslow laid down our basic human needs as food, water, warmth and access to fresh air – the very platform of our survival.

If we think about it, just about everything reverts back to 'have I got something to eat' and 'have I got access to fresh water or air'. For example, If you work in a high-rise building in the summer and it gets warm, one tends to want to open a window, rather than put on air-conditioning. Work is affected, the environment is affected, by those changes.

Once these basic needs are met, Maslow believes we require a sense of safety and security. I'm also going to include love - the right to love and/or be loved.

My interpretation of safety and security is the ability to get 'out of harm's way'. This means to get indoors, to have a roof over one's head, whether that is bricks and mortar, a tent or even – as witnessed by my sons James and Julian when they lived and worked in Thailand – the underside of a vehicle.

James and Julian would watch people on the Khao San road in Bangkok sit for hours waiting for a vehicle to pull up and stop for the night. Then the street dwellers would crawl under the vehicle, ensuring they were 'out of harm's way' from animals, muggers or robbers.

But I would also include here an inner need. Often I'll ask people to describe a 'bolt hole' or place of great peacefulness, comfort, or wellbeing that they experience in life. People will tell me about holidays and places they have visited. Invariably these recollections will contain three ingredients – trees or grass, sea or river, and sky.

If I ask people about indoor retreats, typical examples for men include feet up in front of the TV with a can of beer; for women, a warm and relaxing bath with essences and floating candles; and increasingly for teenagers, their bedroom, with the music on loud in defiance of the world.

When we think that we have these factors in place, Maslow believes that we strive upwards for the next set of needs, which I understand to be belonging.

This is an interesting one. I think there are two sides to it. First, there is the need to belong to a small group within society. For example, as an employee of a city council or county council, it is less likely we feel we belong to the overall organisation than to a department or team within it. Therefore, we feel the belonging to those directly above and below us, those who surround us. This also applies socially. We gain our sense of belonging from being part of a pub darts team, say, or a church congregation. If someone feels that they belong, they feel that they can begin to communicate more effectively.

The second side to it, I think, is 'being seen to belong'. In 1982, I applied to join the Chartered Institute of Marketing, not because I wanted to buy in to or contribute to new thinking in marketing and communication, but because I wanted it to be seen that I associated with it. This is also influenced by factors such as the media, where we are drawn to brands that we believe say something about us, be it clothes, or sports equipment or a car. There is a new materialistic aspect to it.

I think Maslow's point is we then climb to the next level of the hierarchy – self-esteem.

Self-esteem is inner questions such as 'am I a good person', 'am I a good husband or partner or spouse', 'am I a good father or mother'. I believe that I am a good father because both my adult boys tell me, regularly. That's positive affirmation that I continue to need. I did not know that when I was a parent of two growing lads. I had self doubt, no means by which to measure it.

Self-esteem is also asking 'am I good at my job'. As I have

described, I had big troubles with that when I was growing up. I didn't know whether I was or not because of the pressures put upon me, the emotional oppression, as I grew up and went to work. When I look back, on many occasions I was exceptionally good at my job, but I didn't feel it or know it inside at the time. In those days, we didn't have mechanisms such as appraisal systems or feedback. To some extent, it remains a challenging area for me.

Most of the work that I've done over the last 20 years or so in motivating people and teams has been around belonging and self-esteem. When we can get that going positively, big things can happen.

We then arrive at the next-to-the-top part of the hierarchy – self-knowledge, the will to learn.

Self-knowledge is not about forced education. Where there is a will, there is a way. When I first started in training and development 20 years ago, a lot of courses were attended by people who didn't want to be there. There's a phrase 'you can't teach an old dog new tricks'. Well, you can, providing there is a will to learn. Looking back on my education, I never had a will to learn. Nor did I understand about belonging and self-esteem because I'd been bullied and made to feel uncomfortable. Pressures from conditioning as I was growing up made me feel as though I wasn't any good anyway, so I never really got to wanting to learn until much later in life.

These days, when people come to my house for motivation sessions, or I'm running a course, I follow the pathway of the hierarchy in ' breaking the ice'. The first thing we do is to have a cup of tea or coffee, establish whether we have got access to a toilet, when are we going to have a break, when we can talk together without the interference of others. This helps us to own the conversation. I might also run through some exercises to engender a sense of belonging and rapport, so we start to feel more confident in each other.

As soon as these stages are in place, we can get on with learning something new. People can't be forced to learn. During the visits of one of my clients, a gentleman with a stammer, I knew I'd got to concentrate hard. We had our little introduction to my home, including a walk down the garden while keeping up a friendly chat. By the time I had made us both a cup of tea and settled in my study, he said 'this is nice'. That's when I knew we were ready to learn. There is no chance when we feel uncomfortable or insecure.

Self-knowledge can come to any person at any time of life, but only, I believe, when the other needs in the hierarchy have been met. And that takes us up to the pinnacle – aesthetic needs.

These are, to some degree, difficult to describe. It's not materialistic. For instance, I could have two cars, which would satisfy some materialistic need, but I can only drive one at a time. I don't think one can ever get satisfaction from materialistic needs so I tend to look at culture. Age, or length of time, might also have something to do with it.

When I was 50 I took an allotment outside the village. The owners of the land were an older Nottinghamshire couple, I'll call them Margaret and Albert. I'm not sure whether Albert could read or write. The couple had retired and had a pension, so they were financially secure. They owned both the home in which they lived – it was a small static caravan – and the land around them. They did not feel the urge to go away on holidays. They grew a lot of their own food. We could say, therefore, that in terms of food and water, safety and security, everything was taken care of.

So why did they go to Derby Market at 4am every Friday to sell cut flowers? There wasn't a lot of money in it. I believe it was because they're still wanted to feel part of the horticultural fraternity, so people saw and addressed them as fellow growers. It was about belonging and self-esteem. They felt as though they were with their family and friends, acknowledged and recognised.

Albert was continually learning. He didn't have any chemicals on his land and he knew and named all the creatures. He and Margaret kept hens. They tolerated the fact that a male pheasant occupied the same hutch as the hens at night because it liked it in there. Albert grew sunflowers, not as crops, but because he knew the pigeons liked to feed on them. So he was in a continuous learning state. Both Margaret and Albert were satisfying their aesthetic needs and had been most of their life.

My father's golden day was going to be his retirement in the 1980s. Having worked as a butcher for 50 years, he believed that, on his 65th birthday, he was going to have control over his life and his destiny. He had a pension and that's what he had worked for. In 1978, inflation reached 28%. His pension wasn't index-linked. When he retired, his pension had virtually disappeared and he had to continue working until he was 70, as a lorry driver, to secure enough money to survive.

So while I take Maslow's point that it's an upward climb, a climb of hard work, a continuous climb, at the same time I think we can get to aesthetic needs or control at different parts of our lives. And it's not a permanent scenario.

Whereas Maslow in 1963 said everything is a hierarchical climb, I said at the outset of my story in this book 'Rise or fall'. What goes up can come down – at very short notice, when you least expect it.

When I ran the transport company, I imagined I was somewhere around the level of self-knowledge. When I was sacked, within 45 minutes I'd gone down to 'how do we pay the mortgage and feed the kids'. I've been directly 'up and down' this scale at least half a dozen times in the last 20 years.

There have been moments when I've met aesthetic needs, but not very often. Most of the time I've been in a struggle, dealing with 'have I got enough money', 'have I got enough security' and 'what is happening to my self-esteem'. We can try to understand it and learn to manage it as best we can but I don't think, as human beings, we'll be able to say 'OK, I won't have any more self-esteem issues because I've dealt with all of what came before'. I think we're more vulnerable than that – these concerns continually return under different circumstances and timescales for all of us who are, after all, different people.

I'd also break it down into different components, because I find that the 'bottom' end of the hierarchy – such as food and security – are physical needs. If somebody hasn't got any money, it's all right trying to teach them some new skill, but really you've got to try to ensure they've got the support financially before they're capable of accepting the new skill.

Belonging and self-esteem are emotional needs. If our emotions are being attacked or damaged, or as I now believe, oppressed in some way – because they've never been satisfied – then we've got to address that before we can 'move on'.

Self knowledge is educational, or mental stimulus.

Aesthetic needs are intuitive. If I'm struggling with a challenge or a difficulty at the lower end of the hierarchy, that's when I need to be most creative and intuitive, but I find I cannot do it because I'm struggling with the physical aspects. When I'm further up the hierarchy, I'm freed from some worries and constraints. Then I can come up with new concepts.

The hierarchy doesn't take into account the modern desire or aspiration for materialism. Materialism has now entered our lives and shaken up the hierarchy. We believe it's a need, but it's a want, a desire to make us feel better about ourselves.

Where does it come in the hierarchy? Self-esteem? Straight in at number four? There's no sign of money on the hierarchy. Money isn't a motivator. It's not about money. It's about what you want to do with money – or spendability. People believe self-esteem can come from spending. It doesn't, it only goes part of the way.

Maslow chose this hierarchical pyramid and I think it's an unsuitable model now. It's not as strict, rigid or formal as a triangle any more. I think it's a structure of interchangeable shapes, I see them as circles, concentric circles – things go round in different formats throughout life and perhaps reappear in a different form. But it follows a cyclical pattern.

My model would contain Maslow's topic headings. I think we've learned an immense amount from it, but now I see it as a series of inter-related circles or loops that we enter and exit.

I don't want an end result, I'm not saying 'this is the new model', I'm saying 'this is a discussion that can go on and from the discussion we'll carry on discovering more'.

Thank you for reading my book